The Mommie Dearest Diary
Carol Ann Tells All

Rutanya Alda

THE MOMMIE DEAREST DIARY
Copyright © 2013, '15, '20 by Rutanya Alda

All rights reserved.
Photographs from the author's private collection.
No part of this book may be reproduced in any form without permission in writing from the author, except in the case of brief quotations embodied in critical articles or reviews.

Published by the author in New York, N.Y.
Printed in the United States of America
First Edition

Edited by Jeremy Bright

Cover design, portrait, and illustrations by Leon Joosen

ISBN: 978-1-5152-6060-8

For my son, Jeremy—so glad you were born.

For my husband, Richard—peace at last.

"Be in love with yr life"

– Jack Kerouac

"One million dollars: Faye Dunaway. Everybody you can put in this chair will tell you exactly the same thing ... She is just totally impossible. I don't think we have the time to go into all the reasons ... She's just, let's put it, she's just uncooperative ... Ms. Dunaway is for Ms. Dunaway ... She's very unprofessional—difficult woman, really ... keeping actors waiting, keeping crews waiting, all those things."

> – Bette Davis on *The Tonight Show*, 1988, to the question "Who is one of the worst people in Hollywood that you wouldn't want to work with again?"

"He talks so highly of everyone he has ever worked with that I ask him if there is anyone he has not liked. 'Faye Dunaway,' Van Dyke says immediately—but out of the side of his mouth as though he is ventriloquising. 'I think she was on something that made her testy. She was nice to me but she yelled at everybody else.' In his autobiography he describes her as a 'handful.' He played her husband in *The Country Girl*: 'I only agreed to the role because I thought Blythe Danner was going to be my wife,' he jokes today. 'But I got to New York to find that she'd been replaced with Faye. We shot one scene that I thought was my best dramatic work ever. Six weeks later, Faye insisted on reshooting it and I had to go back to New York to redo it.'"

> – Helena de Bertodano interviewing Dick Van Dyke for *The Telegraph*, Jan. 7, 2013

"A gigantic pain the ass ... [Faye Dunaway] demonstrated certifiable proof of insanity."

> – Roman Polanski, as interviewed by Xan Brooks for *The Guardian*, Oct. 7, 2008

Contents

Acknowledgements	i
Foreword	ii
Who Am I, Besides Carol Ann?	1
Life and Love and the Movies	6
The Mommie Dearest Diary	37
Life after Dearest	143

I OWE A debt to my son, Jeremy Bright, for his excellent job editing this book as well as for his honesty and helpfulness. I am also indebted to my friend and fellow Academy of Motion Picture Arts and Sciences member, Leon Joosen, who gave his time and talent for the cover art and illustrations. Furthermore, I am grateful for Tatiana Nuñez and Shade Rupe, whose keen eyes helped proofread.

I would also like to acknowledge and thank my friends for their support and encouragement, especially Christina Crawford and Diane Franklin for their guidance through the world of self-publishing, as well as my wonderful fans and those of *Mommie*, such as the people who packed San Francisco's Castro Theatre on Mother's Day, 2013, for the *Mommie Dearest* gala. It made me realize how many people want to hear these stories and read this diary. You make movies and their magic possible.

ON THE NIGHT *Mommie Dearest* premiered in New York City, I bought my ticket to see the film at the big Loews on Broadway. I sat with trepidation in the back of the packed theater, not because I had an inkling of what was about to happen, but because an actor never knows what will make the cut. Lights out. Projector on. Breath held. It was not long before I was totally taken aback: Not only had many of the intimate moments been cut, leaving the story disjointed and impersonal, but no one could stop laughing—the audience enjoyed the film on a whole other level than a memoir of child abuse could ever intend. It had been conceived and anticipated as an Oscar-winning drama, but arrived as one of the campiest "comedies" of all time, which even Paramount acknowledged by the next weekend, when I heard audiences were already bringing wire hangers and Ajax, by rebranding the promotional material with the invitation to "Meet the biggest mother of them all!"

How did this happen? Where does the blame lie? I don't have a simple answer, but I do have my diary. To my knowledge, there are scant other primary sources for the making of *Mommie Dearest*—a few carefully choreographed press tours, some on-set photos, but no extensive journaling of the day-to-day. And there were a lot of days: I was on location for the duration of filming, from January 1st till wrapping on April 16th, 1981, the day after Faye finished.

People have asked why I didn't make this available sooner. Am I ashamed of the film? No! I love being recognized by fans as Carol Ann. *Mommie Dearest* has become a cult classic, adored by many, most especially its wonderful, loyal fans in the LGBT+ community, but until recently, it never occurred to me that many people would be so interested in how I experienced it.

I'm a private person, and as you'll see, I began keeping this diary to create calmness by bringing order and coherence to my life during rough times. Reliving and sharing some of these memories has been hard for me, but I know it wouldn't be true to the diary to omit anything personal—thoughts, feelings, my own history. So, I have transcribed them for publication with only essential editing for style and clarity. To aid in situating the reader in my life, let me tell you a little about it up until 1981.

Who Am I, Besides Carol Ann?
1942 - 1964

I WAS BORN in Riga, Latvia, on October 13, 1942. I'm dating myself, but that's okay, because my age is on Wikipedia. For Latvians, the war's end brought Soviet annexation, not the promised Allied liberation. Caught in the middle of bitter Russo-German fighting, my mother, grandmother, three-year-old brother, and I were forced to flee in the winter of '45 on a horse cart to the sea. I rode on my grandmother's lap.

Sweden seemed our safest bet with the Baltics occupied in depth by the Red Army. My father, Janis, a poet and lawyer, had sent word for us to evacuate—one of the last things he did before disappearing into the sprawling Gulag "corrective labor" camp system that Stalin had established.

We squeezed onto the deck of a tiny boat set for Stockholm that was overloaded with hundreds of refugees. Halfway, we struck a mine or maybe a torpedo. The ship began to list and sink. My mother grabbed my brother as I sat on our luggage, as I had been told to do, to the extent a two year old can follow orders, and abandoned ship without me. My grandmother, who was seasick in the toilets, had to make her way back for me against the panic, because my mother refused to.

We were rescued by a passing ship with the clothes on our backs and two small suitcases between the four of us, then shuffled around for months in an international game of pass-the-refugees until we arrived in American-occupied Germany, where we were housed communally at the Augsburg-Hochfeld Displaced Persons Camp in the heart of Bavaria. There were many struggles for the stateless among the ruins of the Reich: My memories are mostly of starvation, disease, and all manner of deprivation, as well as the enduring fear of being forcibly repatriated as "Traitors to the Soviet Union." As a child, I saw people commit suicide rather than be shipped back. At six, I helped my grandmother mop blood and brain off our kitchen floor with rags after a man sharing our quarters shot himself in despair. That was my early childhood, terrible certainly, but working on horror films, these gruesome memories were all I needed to invoke feelings of fear and panic for my characters. It's wonderful to have your psychological baggage actually help you at times—it certainly did for me on *Mommie*.

In 1951, after six years on a waiting list, we were granted entry to the United States—the telegram arrived as we were packing to board a ship to Australia, which had offered us asylum the day before. We arrived by transatlantic steamer at Ellis Island, which held, screened, and processed refugees. The Statue of Liberty in New York's harbor looked just as it did on the American postage stamps I had often scrutinized so carefully in the camps.

We needed a sponsor to immigrate—ours was the Presbyterian Church, though we were nominally Lutheran and my mother was one of the least religious people I've known—and there had to be arranged work waiting in America, so that the government would not be burdened by us, and it was similarly made clear that we were not entitled to any government subsidies. The Presbyterians believed that my mother, Vera, and my so-new-that-he-seemed-to-have-just-materialized step-father, Valdis, were predestined to live and work in Arizona, and so we found ourselves in the small city of Flagstaff, population about 7,700, all of whom seemed to think we were Nazis or Communists, or both—but there was no choice, you went where the sponsor sent you.

They worked at a photo shop that they came to own, taking portraits, developing film, and making prints, often through the night, so when they came home they would go straight to sleep. I was also "required" to work there by my parents, unpaid, full-time, apart from school. Like with the sponsorship, there was no choice. That's actually how I first laid eyes upon Joan Crawford in Sedona, Arizona, when I took a photo of her with my Brownie camera as they were filming *Johnny Guitar* (1954). Not to suggest my days were glamorous. On the contrary, I would usually get up early to eat the hardening donut that was left out for breakfast and get myself and my brother ready for school. We had no hot water. There was a wood-burning stove for cooking and boiling tubs of water for a quick bath. There was an oil heater in the small living room, but we were not allowed to light it because that cost money. I had to get on my knees and beg my mother for the twenty-five cents it cost to eat lunch at school. She liked when I groveled. The lunch ladies loved me, because I went back for seconds and thirds and told them how delicious it all was. The other kids thought I was a simple idiot for liking cafeteria cuisine, but they didn't know that was most of the time my only true meal. For dinner we had bread and butter or more donuts. Rarely did my mother cook anything. Once in a while on her day off she did cook, and terribly. I don't know how one can ruin pork chops and potatoes except through cultivated willful ignorance. We survived like this until her mother, Amalija, who assumed all nurturing roles out of necessity, got through immigration control when I was twelve. When we first emigrated, she had been halted for having survived tuberculosis; the x-ray interpreters saw the signature lung scars and sent her back alone across the Atlantic to the D.P. camps for indefinite observation.

My mother was a woman who was quick with the belt. I always had welts on my body that no one saw under my clothes. It's terrible when a parent doesn't love you. You feel worthless. I never understood why until one time, after I had grown up, when she was in a rage and she blurted out in her Bride of Dracula accent that she never wanted me, in fact she had wanted to abort me, but my father had not let her. So there it was. I had to pay the price for being alive.

Since I had no role models in my life, I found them in the movies. For a quarter, I would go to the weekend double feature at the Orpheum Theater at eleven in the morning and not leave till it closed at eleven that night, a craving I fed by secretly saving the street-pennies I searched for during the day. Once, in front of a used car dealership, I found almost a whole dollar in change, and thanked the good Lord for a month of movies. I'd bring some slices of white bread to sustain me with peanut butter if I lucked out. That's actually how I learned to be "American," from that and the radio. I learned manners, and politeness, and how to speak from the various characters whom I got to know. What's more, film helped preserve my sanity by showing that there was more waiting for me in life. I don't know what I would have done if I had no hope of escape. I remember my mother decided she would pay my brother and me twenty-five cents each for cleaning the house. We'd clean it well and work hard all day on our hands and knees, then she would come home and put on her white glove and go along the crevices with a thin finger. If there were any dust, she would have her eureka moment, and give us nothing.

When I turned eleven, my mother decided that she was having a nervous breakdown. She wanted to take a year off from life and go see her friends who had settled on the East Coast. She made arrangements for my brother to go live with our aunt, Mirdza, in Minnesota, and left me in Arizona with my step-father. I suffered a brutal year of molestation. It only stopped when she returned. If I had told her, I knew she would have blamed me. I never told anyone for years, even during years of therapy. I felt so ashamed. When she returned, the two of them beat me. One night, I put a few things in my little book bag and walked down to Route 66 to hitch a ride somewhere, but as I stood there in the middle of the night, I realized I had no money, I knew no one, and I went back.

By twelve, I had gotten a full-time restaurant cashier job at the Ramada Inn, because the manager's wife, Mrs. Renner—who really ran the place—knew me and took pity. Her husband, George, was

German and had endured a similar situation to ours after the so-called Great War. That's really the only money I saw. I went to work from four till midnight and then walked for an hour to get home, because the breaks on the bicycle my brother had occasionally let me borrow gave out as I was going down a hill—my mother didn't take me to the doctor, she just told me that my broken nose "gave me character."

I was always tired in school and once in a while a teacher would catch me napping, but they never tried to figure out what was wrong. Later, when I was in college, I was the assistant manager of the Inn, and I'm not embarrassed to brag that I had the best compliments from guests for my service, so much so that one of the chain's Vice Presidents came up, or down maybe, from corporate to meet me. He offered me a spot in the executive division—no small feat for a woman in 1964—and couldn't believe it when I told him I was planning on quitting soon to go east soon to become an actress. For me, college itself was neither escape nor very enriching. I stayed in Flagstaff and went to Northern Arizona University because I didn't have much in the way of money or guidance. My mother wanted me to become a lawyer and to that end forced me to study economics and marketing. My first class was often at seven in the morning, I would finish my last class around one, and then go study till three, when I went to work and finished at midnight. I would put the top down on my little white Volkswagen Bug to wake myself up in the cold morning to do it all again the next day. What extracurricular time I had, I spent in theatre. I had known that I wanted to be an actress ever since I saw my first play, an adaptation of Anna Brigadere's *Tale of Sprīdītis*, at the age of six in the D.P. camps, so as soon as I finished college, I got on the first plane to New York, feeling free, though my mother would occasionally pick a time to telephone in the middle of the night to tell me things like, "Your brother is the handsome one, he should be the actor. You are too ugly." These calls continued for years until I got an unlisted number.

This was my dear mommie.

Life and Love and the Movies
1964 - 1980

IN ORDER TO SURVIVE New York, I worked as a waitress, drove a Checker cab, and did other odd jobs while I studied acting with great teachers: Lee Strasberg, Stella Adler, Allan Miller, Sanford Meisner, Paul Mann, and my friend and my most influential teacher, Barbara Loden, who was married to Elia Kazan. My first film job was as a high school student in the *Up the Down Staircase* (1967), in which Sandy Dennis played the lead. I worked two weeks and earned enough money to pay a couple of months' rent for my closet-sized, fifth floor walk-up apartment on the Lower East Side, and though I don't remember if my face is even visible, it gave me enough encouragement and happiness to believe that even a life in the background of film beats a life in the background of any other business. It certainly beat busing tables for chump change till four in the morning and struggling to get home.

Strasberg was enamored of me and we dated for a while, but I choked on escargot when he asked me to marry him at Sardi's. I was in my early twenties, naïve, and not prepared to commit to a man whom people consistently mistook for my grandfather. After I said no, he shunned me forever. People often teased that if I had said yes to Lee, I might have been Queen of the Actors Studio. They didn't understand how less-than-thrilling that prospect was.

The two of us did have fun, though. Lee would pick me up in his chauffeured car when I lived in Alphabet City, long before it was chic. He loved visiting the tenement housing because it reminded him of his growing up there as a child—of course, he was now living in a beautiful apartment on Central Park West. He would take me to plays and dinner and back to his place, where like any happy couple we'd spend hours watching bad television and gossiping about people we knew, how Marilyn Monroe, who had studied with his deceased wife, Paula, was "always late to everything" and whenever he ran into her she "reeked of medication." It might surprise many in the Studio to learn that Lee's favorite actor, at least at the time, was John Wayne. Lee expressed enormous delight at the fact that Wayne apparently never formally studied, just as he'd brag that his daughter, Susan, who was older than me and also an actress, had not studied with him, because of her "natural talent."

As a *Mommie Dearest* aside, Lee once took me to an off-Broadway play starring Franchot Tone, who had been married to Joan Crawford, and whom Lee knew from the Group Theater. Franchot dropped his elegant prop walking stick during the play and when we went backstage afterward, he was so upset about the mistake—which probably no one in the audience realized—he just couldn't let it go. Lee said that it was fine and I said that I thought he handled it so adeptly that it was part of the play, and he seemed to feel better. I remember Franchot as being a small man with delicate bones and very delicate fingers and realized when I looked at them that even with his tremendous level of fame and accomplishment, there remained a deep insecurity about his work.

Lee also visited me on the set of *Rosemary's Baby* (1968) and I introduced him to Roman Polanski, to whom I remember Lee being more curt and aloof than I had expected, but Lee was also very aloof and cool to most people he met. For *Rosemary's Baby*, I had been hired as Mia Farrow's stand-in and photo double, and I can actually be seen in all the long and rear shots, except the rear nudity scene that was shot in California—sorry. Very relevant to this book, it was the set where I met Joan Crawford. William Castle, one of the producers, had cast Joan in her later career in some of his horror films, and they remained friends. Castle had asked Joan and actor-dancer Van Johnson to do a cameo appearance in a scene shot at the intimate Sullivan Street Playhouse in Greenwich Village, where "The Fantasticks," an exceptionally long-running off-Broadway musical, was then being performed. Joan arrived wearing a leopard print dress and matching floppy cap that she made elegant, and shortly thereafter came right up to me.

"Hello, I'm Joan Crawford," she graciously said, extending an ungloved hand. "So pleased to meet you."

Startled, I stammered, "Thank you, Ms. Crawford," before processing that because Mia was late and Roman had been shooting me from the back getting out of the cab in Mia's white coat, Joan thought I was Mia Farrow.

Later that evening, Roman was walking back and forth on the set, attending to every little detail, when he overheard Van making Pinocchio jokes to his friend, cinematographer William Fraker, in reference to Roman's prominent nose. "Get off my set," Roman bellowed, and had Van and Joan thrown out, even though Joan had nothing to do with Van's remarks.

As she left, Joan turned and said to Roman, "You should learn to be a gentleman, like Mr. William Castle."

Those kinds of incidents made people cautious and reserved around Roman, which I already had been for a while. There was a scene at the beginning of the script where a young girl commits suicide by jumping out a window, which was omitted from the final cut. The special effects artist had spattered blood all around the dummy corpse lying in front of the Dakota on West Seventy-Second Street. Still, Roman was unhappy because there was not enough. As I stood by, he seized the red bottle and kept screaming, "More blood, more blood," as he Pollocked the sidewalk with it. The next day, Roman inquired, "Why is Rutanya nervous around me?"

Related to *Rosemary* and *Mommie*, in 2013 Roman told Philipp

Oehmke and Martin Wolf for *Der Spiegel*, "I've always gotten along well with women. It was already the case with my second film, *Repulsion*, starring Catherine Deneuve. With her, it was like a tango. The same was true of Mia Farrow in *Rosemary's Baby*. But then I encountered Faye Dunaway when I filmed *Chinatown*. She was very difficult. I nearly came to a halt."

My first real break in film came that same year, when I got cast in two films that a young Brian De Palma was directing starring Robert De Niro, *Greetings* (1968)—distinguished as the first X-rated film in America, in my opinion more for its social commentary than a pair of bare breasts, as there's no pornography—and its sequel, *Hi, Mom!* (1970), which were both original and exciting and celebrated by critics: *Greetings* won the Silver Bear at the Berlin Film Festival, and my performance was prominently reviewed by the New York critics, including then-legendary Pauline Kael, as was my twenty minute scene "Be Black, Baby" in *Hi, Mom!*, which *Life* and *The New York Times* picked for praise. It's worth noting that Brian started out with risqué black comedies, before reshaping his auteurial image as rather Hitchcockian and dramatic. After the two films finished, I ran into Brian and we wound up in bed together. I loved working with him and thought that I could recapture that joy by sleeping with him; and I did get to enjoy working with him again in *The Fury* (1978) and *Dressed to Kill* (1980), in which I did some voice over work, including looping Angie Dickinson's orgasm—take from that casting process what you will.

In '68, I was also hired to be the stand-in for the gorgeous Anne Francis in the film *Funny Girl*. At one point, we would commute daily by ferry from a West Side pier across the Hudson to New Jersey to shoot at a railroad terminal, and the director, William Wyler, would often travel with us—no bodyguards, limousines, or over-inflated ego. Well, at least not his. Anne was a blonde bombshell, at the full bloom of her beauty, and Barbra Streisand, the star, was very aware of how lovely her co-star was. Years later, I heard from Vivienne Walker, the hairstylist on *Funny Girl* and *Mommie Dearest*, that Barbra sat next to Mr. Wyler at all the nightly viewings of the dailies, telling him which beautiful actresses would have their close-ups gone from the film. Thus, Anne Francis received star billing but scarcely appears in the final cut.

Unfortunately, that would not the last time I would work with that diva. I was earning rent and bread as a lowly townsperson in *Hello, Dolly!* (1969), hired for six whole weeks, when Gene Kelly, who was directing, decided extempore that I should also double for Barbra, for we were exactly the same height and size. So, I was dressed in Barbra's costume and you can see me as Dolly in some high angle crane shots and my back in some others, as well as in the long shots of the main song and dance number. At one point, Walter Matthau, a darling man, was shooting a scene with her when, in the middle of filming and in front of the crew and everyone else on set, she broke character and shouted, "Gene, he shouldn't be saying his lines like that!"

Walter glared at her, his face going so red I thought he would explode, "Betty Hutton was once a star, too, and look what happened to her."

"He can't talk to me like that," Barbra screamed and stormed away. Poor Gene. He looked at Barbra's back, then at Walter's face, and made the decision to follow Barbra, because I assume he knew who was the professional and who had to be babied.

After finishing the film, I put all of my Babs records in the dumpster without ceremony. Several years later, I ran into Walter in Los Angeles, and asked if it were true that he blamed the stress of working with Streisand for bringing on his heart attack, as I had heard rumored. "That woman did give me a heart attack," he said, "but I got even with her." He declined to elaborate—I still wonder what he did.

Shortly after completing my work on *Hello, Dolly!*, I learned that my father had survived the Soviet forced labor camps; after Stalin died, Khrushchev had pardoned him with many other political prisoners, but he remained a de facto prisoner behind the Iron Curtain. I spent a long time in bureaucratic hell and my life's savings to go meet him in the Latvian Soviet Socialist Republic in the summer of '69. Though he had not seen me since I was two, I could tell immediately from the way he looked at me, hugged me, kissed me, and cried with me that he loved me—I finally met a parent who loved me, which really meant, and means, the entire world. I returned home to months of American intelligence agents evidently eavesdropping on my calls, poorly, and opening my mail, clumsily, because of the clear and present danger that my daddy issues presented to the United States.

The wonderful director Jerry Schatzberg—who was in a relationship with Faye Dunaway for a while, and whom I later dated briefly—cast me in *The Panic in Needle Park* (1971) and *Scarecrow* (1973). *Panic* starred Al Pacino in his first major film role, as well as my future husband, Richard Bright, who played his brother, though I didn't meet him then, as we did not have any scenes together. *Scarecrow* teamed Jerry again with Al, with the addition of Gene Hackman, both of whom I have a scene with, where I play a hippie who picks them up as hitch-hikers. I recall we were on location at the foothills of the Rockies and the mouth of the Royal Gorge in Canon City, Colorado, where upon my checking into the motel, I found myself next to Gene, unintroduced, who was languidly enjoying a cigar. Trying to break the ice, I complimented him on his choice of smokes, though what I meant was it didn't smell too bad.

"Oh, do you smoke?" Gene challenged.

"Sure I do," I lied.

"Here, have one," he anted. I clipped the tip with his cutter as I had seen people do and lit up my first and only cigar. It only took me a minute to start silently praying to anything listening for the strength to get through this without getting sick all over him. So, we smoked and we talked.

"You're alright," Gene said, and smiled at me. I hurried to my room afterward, spitting on the way, and brushed my whole mouth trying to get rid of the taste. I didn't pack any mouthwash, so I went to the bar and asked for Peppermint Schnapps instead.

Another important film in my early career was *The Long Goodbye* (1973), starring Elliott Gould as detective Philip Marlowe, directed by Robert Altman. I played one of Marlowe's next door hippie neighbors who keeps pestering him with, "Would you like a brownie, Mr. Marlowe?" That was partially my idea. Bob was always open to coworkers' ideas—if he thought you had a good one he'd tell you up front, "I'm going to use your idea but I won't give you credit. I'm going to take all the credit for it."

I had met Bob in New York one day about a year before, shortly after he finished *McCabe & Mrs. Miller* (1971), and were in bed by late afternoon. He was in his mid-forties and I was twenty-nine. Bob was married, but not at all secretive about our affair when he was in the city, though he warned that he would never leave his wife, which I had not even thought to ask. He even introduced me to her at a party and though I distinctly felt she knew what was going on, I was much more uncomfortable with the situation than she appeared to be. He actually did stay married to his wife until his death.

Our relationship lasted about a year-and-a-half. We were a strange combination—which is a nice way to say that we really had nothing in common. His daily schedule included cocaine for breakfast, cocaine for lunch, and cocaine for dinner, plus a lot of booze in between. I had my first and only experience with cocaine through Bob—"here, sniff this"—it made my heart race and I thought I was going to die. It also made me severely depressed for days afterward. My journey in life was to tune in, not tune out; I was in therapy and found any experimentation with drugs to be counterproductive. As a man of excess, Bob also loved to eat. At one point, Bob decided he was getting too fat, yet he "didn't want" to give up the food and the booze, a puzzle he solved with bathroom bulimia. In the middle of all this, Bob would talk to me about having a child with him. Of the many reasons why not that I could have easily given him, I decided the least offensive to his lifestyle and ego was that I honestly didn't want to be a single working mother.

When he asked me to fly out to Los Angeles to work in *The Long Goodbye*, I was excited to go. Although Bob was rather open about our relationship in New York and with his friends, we decided that it would be a good idea to not flaunt it in front of the cast and crew and be very professional. So, on set several men flirted with me, which caused Bob to become very jealous when we were in private. He would punish me by asking lovely young women to join him on the set and go off with his special of the day for a "break," in spite or perhaps because of all the coffee and cocaine. The sign would be that he would take off his big straw hat and put it on the head of his chosen one for the afternoon. I told him later to never put that hat on my head. Ever.

During that time, Faye Dunaway came to visit Bob in his office on Westwood Boulevard. I had first met her at some posh Central Park West party in my twenties, when she had given me her number and asked me to call—I didn't, so she didn't remember me. Bob said she was trying to get a part in another movie he was planning, but he didn't think she was right for it. We were there for hours until something like three in the morning and I was pissed that Bob had not sent her away and was rather enjoying his power position, so I got up and left both of them there. I have no illusions of what happened. The next day, Bob said he was still not going to cast Faye.

Again, that's not to say that he tolerated this kind of behavior himself, or even the idea of it, as was demonstrated when I invited my old friend Haskell Wexler, a great cinematographer, to visit *Long Goodbye*'s set. That didn't go over with Bob, who got deeply and instantly jealous and felt no sense of irony about doing so, so I decided not to do anything on my own after that without Bob's permission, except for one small rebellion.

In the film, Marlowe lives with a beautiful orange cat. He was a "trained" cat, of course, kept in a cage and kept hungry, so that he felt rewarded by being given a tiny bit of food after each good take. I felt sorry for the poor thing, he was meowing all day in his cage for food, so I decided to bring him some chicken scraps one night, which he gobbled up. I don't know how the trainer found out, but he quickly did, and he flew into a rage and demanded that I be fired. Bob just told me to please not do it anymore.

I was looking forward to leaving when I finished my part, but Bob convinced me to stay on and stand-in for the gorgeous Nina van Pallandt, whom he had discovered after she made the cover of *Life* for betraying her ex-lover, Clifford Irving, by outing him as having fabricated the best-selling "autobiography" of Howard Hughes. Bob cast her on a whim after hearing her sing on *The Tonight Show* with Johnny Carson in the wake of the scandal, the song being "You've Got a Friend," which Bob found sickeningly funny. To her credit, Nina was always nice to me. She had rented a house in Malibu and invited me to a party she was throwing along with the rest of the cast. It had a beautiful pool and I had forgotten to bring a bathing suit so I stripped to my underwear, took off my bra, and plunged in. They all thought I was a crazy wild woman—though I wasn't the one betraying my lover and my spouse, I wasn't tripping, and I wasn't even drunk.

I broke it off badly with Bob soon after we wrapped, so perhaps unsurprisingly I am barely in the final cut. Furthermore, near the end of production there was a terrible fight between screenwriter Leigh Brackett and Bob after she told him, audibly, that he had ruined the script. In fact, a lot of other actors would come to join the post-production chorus of "where am I?" In particular, I made a friend of Sterling Hayden in the film, who was wonderful in his role as Roger Wade. From the early dailies we saw, everyone there thought that Sterling would get an Oscar nomination for his work, one which I believe he could have gotten, had his part not been drastically and crudely cut down. Sterling sensed my emotional struggle during the film. We were shooting the beach house scene in Bob's actual house in Malibu and Bob had a fine selection of wines. Sterling selected a bottle and opened it, saying it was really fine wine, and got us two glasses. Bob came in as we were just about to taste and started yelling at me about opening up a very, very expensive one. Sterling said "No, Bob, I opened it. Do you have any problem with *that*?" Bob, a little flabbergasted, actually apologized.

Toward the end Sterling sat me on his lap and gave me advice. "Go out and get lost." What do you mean? I asked. "Go out to a city you don't know, or a part of the city you don't know, and just wander around and get lost. It's good for you. I do it all the time," he said. The last night of the shoot, when I knew my relationship with Bob was done as far as I was concerned, Sterling took me by the hand and we walked on the beach back to his hotel and we went up to his room, which had pages and pages of writing all over the carpet. He told me he was writing a book. He laid me down on the floor near his papers, and after making gentle love to me, Sterling told me of living on his housebarge on the Seine in Paris, where he paid no taxes and lived rent free as an artist. I was invited but, alas, never went.

Later, I saw a production of "A Streetcar Named Desire" at the Dorothy Chandler. Jon Voight played Stanley and Faye of course played Blanche. My friend Paul Zayas was playing one of the card players with Stanley and had invited me to see the play. Paul said

Faye was forever asking him and others for advice on her part. After I saw the play, I went backstage to see Paul, who said lets go to Faye's dressing room and say hello. It was full of people but Paul introduced me, so I said hello. She again had no memory of me; we stayed for a short while and then left.

Shortly after *Mommie Dearest*, I ran into Jon Voight when he was doing "Love Streams" with Gena Rowlands, which John Casavettes had invited me to see. Jon Voight asked me how I liked working with Faye. I just said okay. He volunteered that when he worked with her in "Streetcar," he could never connect with her and had found it a very frustrating experience.

Around that time, I also appeared in two films directed by Paul Mazursky, *Blume in Love* (1973) and *Next Stop Greenwich Village* (1976). If you don't blink you may see me in the party scene in *Next Stop* where the lead actor is trying to raise rent money. John Belushi was one of my acting partners there and he made the couple of days we worked a lot of fun. The party scene was ultimately edited down to a brief minute, though we had a great time filming it, whereas I was completely cut out of *Blume*. I was surprised because the crew loved my scene and I got applause after I finished it. It was funny, but as Paul was to say when he called me: "It took away from the main thrust of the film." I respect Paul for calling me personally and telling me this, he is the only director I have known who respected his actor enough to do this. Paul listened to my story of being re-united with my father in Latvia and was very encouraging by telling me to write about it.

It was on *Blume in Love* that I met director of photography Bruce Surtees. He was crazy about me and the sweetest man ever. He told me he was being pursued by actress and model Valerie Perrine, but he wasn't interested in her—he wanted me, which I couldn't believe. I later quite stupidly broke up with him because I had been so hurt by my recent relationship with Bob Altman, and I was confused by the fact that there was actually a great man interested in me. I didn't think I deserved him and I ran away. In 2012, when I was at the Academy's New York Oscar dinner and Bruce's tribute photo came up on the obituary screen, I couldn't breathe. I hadn't heard. I stopped eating and held back tears, deeply impacted by this sweet man's death.

After *Blume*, Sam Peckinpah cast me in *Pat Garrett and Billy the Kid* because he said I had the bravest audition. I don't know what the others' were like, all I said to my reading partner was not to be afraid to grab or touch me. There was no camera or distance, just Sam and the actors. I had auditioned for the hooker, Ruthie Lee, who gives the Kid up to Pat Garrett because she feels he needs to pay a blood price for having hit her earlier.

We shot in the old city of Durango, Mexico, and walking onto a western set was a dream come true for me: The first movie that I saw in the D.P. camps was a western; the comic books that the American soldiers gave me were of Roy Rogers and Red Ryder; my first English words—of a sort—were "Tom Mix"; and when I got to Arizona, I listened to Johnny Cash when I wasn't at the theater learning English by mouthing dialogue from the latest cowboy B-movie drama-comedy-romance-whatever.

At last, here I was.

I met Bob Dylan on set when he was trying on hats for his character. He looked at me for hat approval and I would silently nod or shake my head, and our relationship on the film developed into variations on a theme. Bob had rented a house in Durango, where he wrote the score, including "Knocking on Heaven's Door." When he would come to the set to see Sam, he would have lunch on set, and often sit with me while never exchanging a word. That was our relationship. Some people thought perhaps there was something going on with us, but he just sat with me because I didn't bother him—though he did allow me to take a photo with him at the end, which at that time was nearly impossible. I saw him several years later at Mink DeVille's show in Los Angeles and he was glad to see me—that time we actually spoke.

On *Pat Garrett*, I would work with my future husband, Richard Bright, for the second time without meeting him. I also hardly saw Kris Kristofferson, as he was not in any of the scenes I worked in, but James Coburn was polite enough, if reserved, as his wife was constantly there keeping an eye on him. She never left.

Unknown to me, Sam had hired real hookers to play the rest of the hookers in the brothel, so when they asked me if I was a working girl, I said "Yes, I work in film and theater." They laughed. I became friends with two of them. One night, Sam decided to have an party in his room at the motel and the girls and I were invited to what turned out to be an orgy, and though I am not exactly a prude, I thought this was a little out of my league as I watched the goings-on. Suddenly there was banging on the door. It was Katy Jurado.

"Sam, don't do this. This is killing you. Don't do this, Sam, please."

"Go away, Katy," Sam screamed back, but Katy persisted and she was loud, which gave me a chance to slip away unnoticed.

Some of the cast of John Wayne's film, *Cahill U.S. Marshal* (1973), were staying at the motel with us. We all ate together in a cafe nearby. Producer Michael Wayne, John Wayne's son, and I became friends and he asked me if I would like to visit the set. Wow. Yes, it would be great to meet the legend. Michael sent a car for me on my day off and on my ride out into the desert I started imagining my coming conversation with John Wayne. Rutanya? That's a strange name. Where are you from? Latvia? That's a Communis' country! Get off my set, you dirty, rotten Red. I scared myself silly.

Upon arriving, I saw him coming straight toward me. I started shaking. This was it.

"Hi, I'm John Wayne," he shook my hand. "How do you walk in them thar things?" He pointed at my clogs.

"The same way you walk in your big boots, Mr. Wayne." He laughed and laughed like I had told him the funniest joke.

"Come on over here," he said, walking me to the food wagon. "You look like you could use a good meal"—I was very thin at the time—"Let me know if you need anything," and off he went. I've never been on a set where it felt more as if I were being hosted in someone's home, he was that gracious and kind to everyone. I learned that he loved to play chess and there was a man he hired just to play with him, so when John had a break from shooting he would head for the chess table. His concentration was amazing. Throughout the day he would check in with me, "You okay? Need anything? How you doin'?"

Moreover, John did something I have never seen a star do: After finishing a shot, he turned to the director and pointed to the other, less known actor, "Give him the close-up." I was so impressed that I vowed if I were ever in that position, I would do the same thing and I did when starring in *Amityville II* (1982). Danny Aiello, Jr., was cast as the handyman who comes to the basement to check on the fly infestation. They were shooting him from the back and the side, so I turned to the director and said, "Give him the close-up," and he got it. I was so happy to be able to pass that on.

Sam found out about my visit to the *Cahill* set and arbitrarily considered me a "traitor" and let everyone know about it—it made no sense, but he was determined to make my life on set miserable afterward by taking every opportunity to allege that I didn't want to be on his set and that I'd rather be working with Wayne. Still, that wasn't as bad as some experienced, as Sam would often ask people to tell him what they really thought about something, but if you said the opposite of what he said, you were devalued at best and fired at worst. One quickly learned that when asked, always agree with Sam.

Another actor on Sam's set was John Barrymore, Jr., who was very thin and fragile-looking. He helped me with my shoe when I lost it and felt for a minute as if I were Cinderella. I would meet him again later when John started living with my downstairs neighbor in Hollywood. I came home one night to find smoke coming from his apartment. I shouted, but there was no answer. I tried the door, found it unlocked, and rushed in. Everything was smoke. I found John passed out on the couch and I dragged him outside into the fresh air and put out the kindling fire on the couch and rug below. John revived, fortunately unburnt, but coughing as if he had bad bronchitis. This was a couple of years before Drew was born, and I've always felt that if I or someone else hadn't been there to save him, their Hollywood dynasty could have ended then and there.

The man occupying the room next to me in the motel in Durango was actor Neville Brand, one of the stars of *Cahill*. Neville became smitten with me and we became lovers for the duration of the month in Durango. Neville and I would dine in a very romantic setting at the restaurant La Casa Blanca and we would walk and talk a lot. He was an avid reader and would tell me the stories of the books that he had read.

We would also walk through the Durango graveyard where a lot of Americans had been buried at the turn of the century and would take turns in making up stories about their lives, what they had been doing there, how they died. It was fun to let our imaginations soar, and it was something to do outside of the cantinas, for Neville had given up drinking as it had nearly destroyed him and his career. He was grateful to Lew Wasserman, the big boss of Universal Studios, for personally helping him through his alcoholism. He had lost his driver's license and rode his bike, his only mode of transportation, around Malibu where he lived. For a while he also had been rendered impotent and the fact that he could now perform again with me took him by surprise and he was thrilled.

He rented Dolores Del Rio's former residence for a good view of a big parade in town, which was beautiful and romantic, and Dan Kemp from his film joined us there and many days after that as we wandered around. Dan and I and Neville all became very close friends. One day we all went into a church and I got Neville to say a prayer with me. Dan said he would never forget the sight of Neville on his knees in church, because he had given up his godbelief during the Second World War. Neville was a highly decorated combat infantryman and I knew firsthand that he still had nightmares of the people whom he saw die and had killed.

Neville told me he loved me. There was a problem though: He was married with teenage children. He seriously considered giving up his life and making a life with me. After the film was over and we were both back in Los Angeles, Neville called me to come over. His wife and children were out and we made love on his bed, which I must say was a very uncomfortable situation for me. Neville wanted to continue to see me but in the end he didn't want to give up his comfortable life with his family, Malibu home, and big boat. I left that day affirming that I would stop seeing him—I had to be worth more than that.

Another film I did in 1973, *Executive Action*, had a really interesting script that dealt with theories of John F. Kennedy's assassination. The screenplay was written by the great Dalton Trumbo, who had been one of the Hollywood Ten and blacklisted for years, though he still won an Oscar for Best Original Screenplay for *The Brave One* (1956) using a fictitious name. I had met Dalton a few years before at the Algonquin Hotel in New

York, after he had just made *Johnny Get Your Gun* (1971), a moving anti-war film that profoundly affected me. The premise of *Executive Action* is that a group of Texas businessmen, led by Burt Lancaster and Robert Ryan, conspire to assassinate the President, and I was cast as part of the assassination team. My friend, John Brascia, who was a very well-known dancer and the partner of Vera Ellen in *White Christmas* (1954), was on the team too, trying to switch to dramatic acting. One day, Johnny came in and told me he had spent the evening at his friend Fred Astaire's house. They were playing pool when Fred got inspired and jumped up on the pool table, took the cue and danced with it while he kicked each ball into the pockets with his feet. I was in gaga-land listening to him.

Before I was cast in this part, I had auditioned for *Serpico* (1973) for the role of Serpico's girlfriend. I had a great meeting with Sidney Lumet, the director, and we must have talked for about an hour. Several weeks went by and I didn't hear anything, during which I was cast in *Executive Action* to shoot in Los Angeles. A few days into the shoot, my agent calls to tell me that Sydney wants me for the part in *Serpico*, which I now couldn't do as I was on contract. It's one of those times in my life when my career might have taken a greater path, for *Executive Action*, which was shot in secrecy due to the producers being quite worried because of the subject matter, faded away quickly in the box office and *Serpico* became a great hit.

One good thing came out of my time in California, though: I got to know Richard Bright, my future husband. I was living in Los Angeles when he came to shoot *Marathon Man* (1976) and he called to have coffee. Richard was the most authentic person I knew, a breath of fresh air from all the Hollywood artifice. You never had to second guess what he meant, if you asked him for an opinion he gave it to you frankly. He was also just a fun person, with a great gift of humor and storytelling, strengthened by his avid reading and foreign film watching. We saw every foreign film available in Los Angeles and discovered a Japanese theater on Crenshaw that had a double bill of new films every week.

I hung out with him and Sir Laurence Olivier on the set of *Marathon Man*. Richard was in admiration of "Larry," as Sir Laurence had asked Richard to call him; they would continue to correspond as friends long after production ended. Sir Laurence was very much the gentleman: Though he was suffering from health issues, one being that touching him put him in incredible pain, he reached out and touched me, or anyone he met, ever so gently. Richard was upset with Dustin because he would make Sir Laurence go on and on for hours in rehearsal though he was not in great health and touch him unnecessarily, but Sir Laurence never complained. I told the director, John Schlesinger, my favorite moment in his many great films was in *Far from the Madding Crowd* (1967), when the coffin is going down the hill and the dew from the leaves drop on it—it was like the trees wept for the deceased, that they were the only ones weeping for her. John was startled. He was quiet for a moment and then told me that it was his favorite moment, too, and that no one had ever said that to him before.

After a couple of months, *Marathon Man* wrapped, so Richard decided to stay on and look for new work in Los Angeles. We had been best friends for a year-and-a-half before we became intimate, and soon decided to marry. We also decided to move back to New York. Richard never told me about his drug past, heroin being his poison of choice. I think that even if he had, I wouldn't have understood the implications of what that meant.

With *The Fury* (1978), I got to work again with Brian De Palma. Kirk Douglas starred, Amy Irving was the female lead, Frank Yablans of *Mommie Dearest* was the producer and always a gentleman to me, but perhaps most importantly, the legendary William Tuttle was the makeup person, and he said that I had great brows. He had been the makeup artist to many stars, as far back as Jeanette MacDonald. When she died in 1965, she had requested in her will that he make her up for the funeral, though he didn't want to, as he had never made up a dead person before. Yet, out of respect for her, he did it, and explained to me how the artistry was totally different and it was like going back to school to hide the decomposition effects, such as blackening of the skin. At one point, Amy Irving came back from a weekend of sunbathing with screaming red skin, which made Bill furious. He thought she was unprofessional and uncaring. He had to match her skin tone from the last take, while making her skin seem natural and seamless, which would take hours of work to do, not to mention that she was bound to start peeling soon. John Cassavetes was also in the film. We had not seen each other since *Rosemary's Baby*, and as we rehashed old times, I found out that he had hated Roman Polanski and working on it.

On the heels of that, *The Deer Hunter* (1978), another film of mine, won the Academy Award for Best Picture. It remains a great story of the rituals of life: weddings, wars, and funerals. Centered on a group of friends in a small town whose lives are forever changed by the Vietnam War, I played Angela, who marries John Savage's character and whose life is destroyed by her husband's severe psychological and physical service injuries. She has shut down and is unable to speak, listening to a hand held radio as her only nostalgic comfort, when Robert De Niro's character returns home from the Army to ask her where his old friend is—her shell of a husband.

I loved working with Michael Cimino, the director and writer. He was intense and supportive of his actors. John Cazale and I also became close friends on the film. We were both news junkies and would read the newspaper at breakfast to each other after working eighteen hour days. We would pick out stories of interest and would read them out loud and discuss them and we would continue following the details even during our time in the makeup chair. We discussed his bout with lung cancer as well, and he was convinced that he had beaten it and was telling everyone who smoked to please stop before they weren't as lucky. During the funeral scene, Cleveland was in a historic heat wave and we had on heavy woolen clothing, so in the bar scene at the end, still in wool, John and I would go into the walk-in refrigerator and sit on cases of Rolling Rock bottles to cool off. We would come out of the walk-in with our clothes literally steaming, but cool and ready for the next take. I also made life-long friends with the wonderful actor, George Dzundza. Still to this day when I see or drink a Rolling Rock beer, I think of sitting on those cases in that refrigerator with Johnny.

Later, I was downstairs at my friend and fellow actor, Howard Rollins' apartment watching the Academy Awards when John Wayne announced *The Deer Hunter* as Best Picture. Howard and I rose up out of our chairs and whooped it up and ran around his apartment screaming and shouting. How ironic that I didn't work for nearly two years afterward. This is the life of an actor. It's very often feast or famine. I heard from Michael that when he was in the elevator with Jane Fonda, who had won the Oscar for Best Actress, she snubbed him for beating her *Coming Home* (1978), because he had somehow accrued a reputation for not being sufficiently anti-Vietnam, but how anyone could see *The Deer Hunter* and not grasp that it is profoundly anti-war is beyond me.

When I next worked, it was as Mrs. Mandrakis, the mother of the murdered children in *When a Stranger Calls* (1979), with Carol Kane. Doug Chapin, who had been my fellow actor and neighbor on West Eighty-Fifth Street in New York, was producing and was a friend to both myself and Carol and had me in to read for the part. One of my scenes that was cut out showed me—spoiler alert—a year after the deaths of my children as a catatonic mess.

I also played the doctor who delivers Rocky and Adrian Balboa's baby in the *Rocky II* (1979). I had gone in to audition for Sly Stallone and was nervous. He said to me you shouldn't be nervous after all the films you have done. He said too bad you didn't come in for the original *Rocky* and audition for Adrian. Duh! I had tried so fucking hard to be seen for that part, it really hurt to hear that now.

About a year before I was cast in *Mommie*, I came home early and unexpected from a shoot to find my husband with a needle in his arm. I was stunned. I had been totally clueless. I didn't understand what it meant to be an addict. He finally told me about his past and his struggle to stay clean. I thought once you were clean you were past that, but no, every day was a struggle. I thought you could just stop. I was ever so naïve. But I had taken my marriage vows very seriously and was committed to helping him. His sobriety would work for a while, sometimes six months, but then it would flare up again. The interesting thing was if Richard were working, he was sober. He loved to act. He was a great talent, amazing to watch as he was connected to his instincts and would be very brave in his choices. When he was on stage you couldn't take your eyes off of him. He was exactly the kind of actor Elia Kazan loved, because there was a certain danger in his work. Richard would do the unexpected. His performance was not predictable like so many today. But so many days in an actor's life are spent not working and those are the dangerous days. The heroin addiction flared up again and again. Our finances were being wiped out. Richard would swear that this was it, but of course it wasn't. There were months and months when Richard was clean and sober and went to therapy and I thought we had made the breakthrough. It was like a demon that wouldn't die.

That brings us to *Mommie Dearest*, where my life intersects with Carol Ann's. My diary is unabridged because I think that is the best way to understand my experience, how the terrible tension in my marriage made the yelling, temper tantrums, and chaos on set sometimes seem like a vacation from my own private miseries, as well as the daily difficulties, struggles, and power relationships of making movies, and thereby a sense of the strength it took for Joan to become the Hollywood royalty that she was and remains.

Clockwise: Me, c. 1949, in a dress my grandmother made from scraps; my mother, Vera, c. 1940s; my first performance, singing "O' Christmas Tree" in memorized English for American delegates in the D.P. camp in Germany; and my father, Janis, and I in 1980, in the Soviet Union, a year before he died.

Clockwise: Altman with friend at his house, part of the set of *The Long Goodbye* (1973), wearing his infamous straw hat; photo-doubling for Streisand in her Dolly costume, designed by Irene Sharaff, after being upgraded by Gene Kelly; and as a townsperson in *Hello, Dolly!* (1969) wearing Judy Garland's costume from *Meet Me in St. Louis* (1944), also designed by Irene Sharaff, which sold for thousands of dollars at a Beverly Hills auction that I attended. I told the auctioneer "I wore that." He rolled his eyes, "I'm sure."

Sam Peckinpah and I on location for *Pat Garrett and Billy the Kid* (1973); my boyfriend, Neville Brand, and I, watching a parade in Durango, Mexico.

Burt Young and I, posing on the set of *Amityville II: The Possession* (1982); Elia Kazan sent his book to me, unsolicited, with this wonderful inscription. His wife, Barbara Loden, was my dear friend and best teacher. I still miss them.

Top, left to right: Michael Cimino, John Savage, John Cazale, and George Dzundza on the set of *The Deer Hunter*, in which I co-starred as Angela, the wife of Savage's character. The wedding scene was shot under hot lights and with no air conditioning during a summer heat wave. No one's clothes were ever dry, as one can see from the men's shirts. *Bottom:* My first glimpse of Joan Crawford on the set of *Johnny Guitar* (1954), I took the photo but didn't meet her until 1969; Kukums and I at the Chateau Marmont.

Hairstylist Vivienne Walker and I on the set of *Mommie*; Joanna McClure, Michael McClure, and Richard at the Marmont.

On set with visitors, Faye was gracious about taking impromptu photos, but guests had to be cleared with her first on days when she was shooting; Harry Goz and I on set at the Beverly Hilton Hotel for the wedding scene, Frank Perry removed me at Faye's request because I "looked too good."

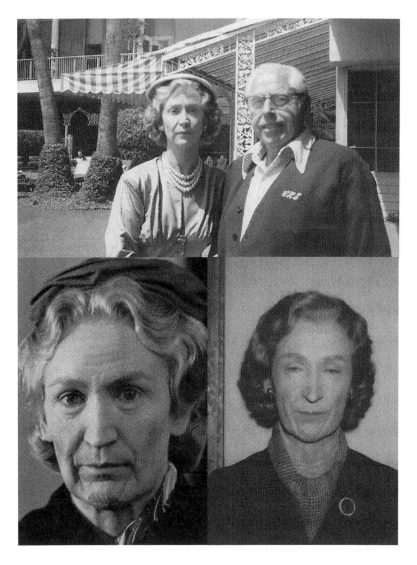

Makeup artist Charles Schram and I on set at the Beverly Hilton Hotel; my late stage makeup and neck application; and my final stage of old age makeup and hat that I was supposed to wear for the funeral scene, but they couldn't find it and instead brought me a floppy hat that was way too small, which I refused. Charlie said he derived inspiration for my look from Georgia O'Keeffe.

Frank Perry, who really chopped down the tree, because Faye wasn't strong enough. You can spot the noticeably different chops in the inserts.

Top, left to right: Frank Perry, Steve Forrest, I, and Frank Yablans on set. People would remark what a happier set it was when Faye wasn't there. This was the first day I saw Frank Y. not in an expensive suit. Also, note Steve's twin cigarettes. *Bottom:* Playing cards. Frank Y., who is up $780,000, is told, "You own my house, my car, my mother." Frank says, "You can keep your mother."

Top, left to right: Mara Hobel and I; from the deleted scene where Carol Ann first speaks to Joan in her car as a super-fan. "Carol Ann, are you here again?" "Oh yes, Ms. Crawford, I'll always be here for you." "Do you want to come work for me? Get in." *Bottom:* Faye and I, festively frumpish.

Top: David Koontz, Christina Crawford, and I after the film at their home. *Bottom:* Betty Barker, Joan Crawford's real long-time secretary, and I. We met after the film was completed, though I spoke with her on the phone before we started filming. She was very friendly and polite to me, but also very guarded and general with personal information about her time with Joan and we never had a significant conversation. The character of Carol Ann is an amalgamation of historical people, such as Betty, and Frank Perry and Frank Yablans' own creativity with reimagining the text. Christina Crawford later told me that she and her brother, Christopher, detested Betty, "She lied about us and was always making trouble."

The Mommie Dearest Diary
1981

Notes from December, 1980

A WEEK BEFORE CHRISTMAS, I get a call from my Los Angeles agent, Kendall Giler. I have an appointment the next afternoon to audition for Frank Perry in New York. I'm to meet him at his Park Avenue apartment at two. I am nervous because I'm always nervous for appointments. There is no script. I will be meeting with Mr. Perry and we will "talk." I like that. The old time directors, the great ones, always met with you personally and got a sense, a feeling about you. I remember my meeting with Elia Kazan for *The Last Tycoon* (1976). He was the only one present. There were no casting people, no producers, no other people. Just him and me. When I met Kazan, he sat at the end of a very long room, and as I walked in, I could feel him literally taking in my being. He made up his mind about me during the walk. I sat down and he told me I was hired. I was totally shocked and elated beyond words and I burst into song walking down the Paramount lot afterward.

There were only a few other times that that ever happened. *Greetings* was Brian De Palma's early comedy and he hired me after I did some improvisation that he thought up. Then, when I met Michael Cimino for the part of Angela in *The Deer Hunter*, we spoke for maybe fifteen or twenty minutes and I got hired without an audition. When I met Michael, it was just the two of us in the room again. On my way out the door after the meeting, I was so excited I opened the wrong door and found myself standing in a dark closet. After a few seconds, I had to open the door to exit and I saw Michael's face. "I'm in the closet," I said. He was amused, so I found the right door and exited. Or, maybe that closet was the right door in the first place—it certainly had him see me in another light.

So, I'm to meet the director, Frank Perry. Will he be by himself or will there be an entourage? The wind is gusting and I am freezing on my way to Frank's. I'm wearing a black knee-length skirt and a red sweater. It's pretty, but it isn't warm. I am chilled and shivering as I go up the elevator and get out. Frank is waiting for me. He helps me with my coat and scarf and we settle down across from each other. I rub my hands together to get warm and hope that my ice cold hands haven't given him a bad feeling. It is just the two of us. I am a little tongue tied, but know I'd better say something. "Hi."

Frank is most gracious, a great host in his home and trying to make me feel comfortable. We share a few stories, and then he starts to tell me a little about the character of Carol Ann. She is Joan Crawford's faithful assistant, helper, baby sitter, and best fan. My imagination catches right away as we talk about that kind of loyalty. I see an imaginary situation and point it out to Frank and even speak about it from Carol Ann's point of view. I see his eyes light up and he says yes, yes, exactly. But Frank says, "That's good, let's save it." He doesn't believe in rehearsing it. He believes that you save it for the camera, because that's where it matters. He thinks that if one wastes those moments in rehearsal, they'll never come back in the same fresh way.

My meeting with Frank lasts about thirty minutes. He cues me when our time is over, and I know that someone else will be on their way up shortly. He helps me again with my coat and scarf and thanks me so much for coming. As I look into his beautiful big brown Bambi eyes, I know that he had meant it. He is sincere. I feel good going down and into the street. The cold air hits my being with a blast as I hurry crosstown, where I am to meet my husband, Richard Bright, for a bite to eat. Afterward, as we walk up Eighth Avenue to catch a bus home, I speak of the audition some more. I forget exactly what I said, but Richard jumps on me for not saying other things that he thinks I should have said. The "should haves" come pouring out of him. I start to cry. Not little tears, but big wailing sobs that come right from my gut. "I did the best I could," I sob. "I didn't think of those things." Richard realizes what he has done. He apologizes immediately and I work on pulling myself together, not caring about the stares I am getting from passersby.

The next morning, I come down with the worst flu I had ever had. My temperature is 104 degrees Fahrenheit and my body is racked with chills. I can't get warm enough even with five blankets on me. I am sick like this even on Christmas Day. And then the phone rings—it's Frank wishing me a merry Christmas and telling me I got the part. As sick as I am, I don't dare tell him that I'm feeling awful. I feel vulnerable and the thought of being fired because I am sick enters my feverish mind. I'm so happy that I had got cast. I am to leave on New Year's Day for Los Angeles, as the wardrobe and screen testing will start the day after. I just pray that I will make it physically, I have never been this sick in my adult life. I can barely move just to go to the bathroom, but I accept the job. A calm settles over me, as I know I just have to rest now and get well enough to travel come January.

I am booked to live at the famous Chateau Marmont in Los Angeles for the indefinite duration of the film. I had driven by that place so many times when I lived in L.A. I've always wanted to stay there, but it's been beyond my budget. At last, months at the Marmont. It's wonderful. I'll fly alone. Richard will come later, after he's made arrangements to bring our cat, Kukums, with us.

(He was a black and white beauty who found me one day during a huge rainstorm in New York and followed me home. He had been very sick and recovered sleeping on my bed for a solid week. He was the smartest, most fearless cat I've ever had, and we made quite an entrance at the Marmont's gardens and pool, as I put the leash on him and he went out for his daily constitutional.)

Thursday, January 1st, 1981

I arrive at the Los Angeles Airport. I am picked up by a driver from Holland who drives for *Playboy*'s limousine fleet. The lobby of the Chateau Marmont is beautifully decorated and the Christmas tree that greets me is spectacular. I am checked into room thirty-five, a one-bedroom suite. A beautiful bouquet of flowers and a fruit basket await me with a card from Frank Yablans, the producer, saying "Welcome aboard." So, Frank Y. is the producer and Frank P. is the director. It's Frank and Frank, two Franks I like very much.

(I had met and worked with Frank Yablans before. He was a class act producer, who was a rare bird in the business. He returned phone calls personally. It came from a time when he was on the road a lot earlier in his career making calls and having to wait in his hotel room for people not returning his. He had been president of Sigma 3, a small distribution company and a branch of Filmways, who had released Brian De Palma's *Greetings* and its sequel *Hi, Mom!* I was in both films. I had met Frank when I tried to get the clips of my scenes to show agents I was trying to get at the time. Finally, I did get the clips after Frank made me swear that they were for my personal use only. In '78, I did a third film with Brian that Frank produced called *The Fury*, at the end of which Frank gave us each a gold necklace with a plaque in the center that read "The Fury." Mine was stolen by my downstairs klepto neighbor a few months later. Not that I was too keen on wearing it.)

Friday, January 2nd, 1981

My call is to be at Paramount at 9:00 a.m. The company has rented me a snazzy blue-and-white Mustang, so I get to drive myself there, what fun. I get there early, Frank and Frank are not in yet. I speak with Robin and Carol Ann, secretaries to Frank Perry and

Frank Yablans. (I wonder if that is how they got the name of Carol Ann for the film.) The assistant director Michael Daves and hairstylist Vivienne Walker arrive at 9:30. Wardrobe comes at 9:40. I make an appointment to meet with Vivienne for wig fittings at her place in the Valley at noon. I go to the wardrobe to be measured and try on costumes until 11:15.

Then I go downstairs to see Frank Perry. He asks me to think about where in the script I become aware that Joan's punishment is becoming too excessive. Also, at what time in the script do I become the mother to Joan? These are good questions and I start thinking about them and continue to all the way on the drive to Vivienne's for the wig fittings. Vivienne has a remarkable hair studio at back of her house in a converted garage filled with hundreds of beautiful wigs, hand-made with real hair and worn by the big stars of the day.

Charlie Schram, the makeup designer, is there. His career spans back to *The Wizard of Oz* (1939). It seems that he has come out of retirement and so has Vivienne to work on this picture in particular—they have both worked with the real Joan Crawford several times and knew her quite well. They both liked her very much and said that she was the most gracious person, knew everyone's name, remembered everyone's birthdays, and sent out personally signed cards. Vivienne said she regularly got cards and phone calls from Joan, when she was alive. I leave there at 2:30 to have a bite to eat and back at the Paramount Studio from 4:30 to 6:30 for wardrobe fittings.

Saturday and Sunday, January 3rd and 4th

I read, read, and read some more. Frank gave me books on Joan Crawford and I had bought her biography in New York and started reading it on the plane. I immerse myself in the readings. I don't leave the room at all, just have a little room service when I get hungry to the point of distraction.

Monday, January 5th

I have lunch with my agent, Kendall, then finish the book *Mommie Dearest* by Christina Crawford. I bring all the books back to Frank Perry. Frank and I discuss the makeup Charlie is planning for my character's aging during this thirty-year period. We discuss Carol Ann and her background. I decide she works in a secretarial job close to M.G.M. and so my character, Carol Ann, can be there during all her free time to ask for autographs from her idol, as Joan Crawford was then signed with M.G.M. Frank tells me I look great, very pretty, like a leading lady. I tell him I dressed up for lunch with my agent. Frank says it works, but to not look this good for Faye, she might feel threatened. I tell him not to worry, I'll wear my fluffy pumpkin pants that don't flatter me at all. I pick up my per diem. I run into actor Ed Begley and his wife, Ingrid, and we have dinner at El Coyote. Time to head home.

Tuesday, January 6th

I again meet Charlie Schram, the main makeup man at Paramount. He is to make a life mask of me. This is a two-step process: First, some ecru paste is spread all over my face, including my eyelids. The mouth is completely covered and so are the ears and neck, but there are uncomfortable tubes up my nostrils to breathe. Then, the plaster is put over this, which gets very heavy, and takes about thirty-five minutes. I wasn't supposed to move at all. I am claustrophobic. My heart starts to beat two-hundred beats a minute, I'm sweating, I'm absolutely terrified. Charlie won't take no for an answer. He is a matter of fact kind of guy. He's here to do the mask, do it and get out. Forget how I feel, that's not his concern. I'm not supposed to move at all.

I keep telling myself I can get through the worst thirty-five minutes ever, as he counts them down in intervals, and I endure until the last four minutes. I'm still suffering from the after effects of that horrible flu. It has left me with fatigue and a terrible cough that has not gone away. The last four minutes I have to cough but I can't, because the heavy plaster totally sealed my mouth. The plaster on my face and neck weighs like a well-fitting cinder block. The cough gets choked up in my chest and suddenly I can't breathe. I start feeling faint and I think I'm going to pass out. I grab Charlie's arm and try to tell him in gestures what's happening to me, or at least panic. He says in a very firm, maybe (a little?) nasty voice that I have to hold still, otherwise all his work to this point will be ruined and that will be my fault.

I grab at his hand thinking I'm going to pass out. I feel like I am suffocating and am going to die. I try grabbing the mask, but Charlie restrains me. I manage to suck in a very shallow breath of air through the straws in my nose, while suppressing this cough that's now stuck rattling around my chest with no exit. Charlie tells me to hang on and then within a couple of minutes he starts peeling the mask off. It went well except for a crack across the neck, but it is a clean crack and apparently routine so Charlie fixes it. I gulp in fresh air and cough like crazy for a couple of minutes. Charlie pays no attention to me. He seems very annoyed.

(The process has become much faster and easier and the materials much lighter to work with. In 1993, I had a life mask done for George Romero's *The Dark Half* that was an entirely different experience. I also told the makeup man about my claustrophobia, and he informed me that it was now no problem for him to do half of the face at a time.)

From there, I check in with production and they don't need me. I have lunch at Oblatt's, a restaurant right at the entrance to Paramount, and then start coughing all over again. I make an appointment with my internist in L.A., Dr. Shere, to check my lungs on Thursday. I go back to the Marmont and take a nap, then read the script again, reread it once more, watch a little T.V., sleep.

Wednesday, January 7th

Call my dentist, Dr. Chin, to make an appointment for both Richard and myself, when Richard gets in. I drive out to meet my friend, Dory, at her house in the Palisades, her husband Frank Pierson is there too. I do errands afterward. Back home at 6 p.m. Carol Ann called from Frank Yablan's office and said the new script is ready tomorrow and they'll send it to me by messenger. The too loud, too sensitive fire alarm goes off twice from cooking on the stove in my room at the Marmont. Scares me like crazy.

Thursday, January 8th

Go to Dr. Shere to check out lungs, feel light headed and weak. He wants me to get plenty of rest and do nothing for at least four days. He says this was a wicked flu and to take antibiotics. I come home and rest all afternoon and evening.

I try calling unemployment in Sacramento to straighten out some of my missing past checks. No answer anywhere. Finally left a message to call me. Unemployment is the life of an actor, and unemployment insurance is what gets us by in our careers.

New script is delivered that I read and reread.

Friday, January 9th

Unemployment lady calls early in the morning. I'm to put in for missing checks. I'm going to get some sun by the pool. Heal. Heal. Later I go to the local unemployment office to fill out all the paperwork to file for missing checks, then gas up, stop at the bank, and meet my friend Jane H. at her house to go see *Inside Moves*, a new film starring Diana Scarwid, who is to play the older Christina. It is strange to see her be John Savage's girlfriend, when I remember playing his wife for all those weeks in *The Deer Hunter* just a couple of years ago. I feel a kind of pang in my chest, I guess the way an ex-wife would feel when she sees her ex-husband with a new girlfriend. Diana obviously has done a terrific job.

I go to Jane's afterward to talk. She gives me her newly written script to read. I finally arrive home at 3 a.m., way too late for my schedule. I had called Richard earlier. Well, I had to call my next-door neighbor in New York, Denise, to tell Richard to get off the phone so I could talk to him. He sounded angry about having to take down the Christmas tree by himself and also about coming out to Los Angeles. Something in me tells me that it would be better for me if he didn't come, but I can't get those words out. I wish I could say that. I want to call him back and tell him, please don't come—I'm actually happy for the first time in ages, I need all my energy for Carol Ann, for the film. When he comes it will all be all about him. But I don't have the strength and courage to do that. I know if I do I will be in for a huge, tumultuous, long-distance fight. So I silence myself and I swallow the pain and I let this happen. This has become a pattern for me, choking back my feelings, silences. I know this is not good.

Saturday, January 10th

David Garfield (John Garfield's son) calls me up to invite me to dinner at his house. I can't because I'm going to my agent's for dinner. I feel very bored and lonely today. I go down by the pool to get some sun, reread the script again and again, and also read Jane's script to change pace before dinner at Kendall's.

Sunday, January 11th

Call my husband in New York. I still am not brave enough to tell him not to come. He will accuse me of having an affair and it will get messy. I just need time to concentrate on my part. I reread my scenes and the entire script again. Need a break. Take an aimless drive around L.A., get a taco and burrito. Driving around L.A. is kind of a mindless meditation. Given how many people meditate daily here, maybe that is why one hears of so many bad accidents.

Monday, January 12th

Mauri from the production office calls early to schedule a wig fitting at 11 a.m. at Paramount. I go in, Charlie Schram is there. The first piece looks good. I look at and study more of Joan Crawford's pictures that they had available there. Lunch at Oblatt's. My commercial agency, Herb Tannen's, calls with an audition that I actually have time to make. After talking about my role on *Mommie Dearest*, I arrange to meet them and sign a new three year contract.

Met Gita Breslin at the Writers Guild for screening of film 9 to 5. It was fun going with her, as Gita had worked as being a stand in for Jane Fonda on many of her films and was also her personal masseuse. She told me they had broken their relationship when Gita had somehow gotten injured on Jane Fonda's film set and filed for disability insurance and Jane had gotten very angry at Gita for doing that. Jane never hired Gita again.

Tuesday, January 13th

First a medical exam for insurance purposes for the film. The doctor really sticks this metal instrument up my nose. Both nostrils hurt like hell and hurt for the rest of the day. I guess he was checking for cocaine usage. Well, I passed, as I have been a person whose life-long search has been for clarity and I learned early on that drugs interfere with that.

I have a wardrobe fitting with Irene Sharaff. She is a great costume designer and a five-time Academy Award winner, who has worked with dozens of the legendary stars. The real stars. The stars from the '30s and the '40s and the '50s. She is a legend in this business and has come out of retirement to do this film, for she costumed the real Joan Crawford numerous times. She is marvelous and has a great eye. Among hundreds of costumes, she effortlessly and quickly picks out things for me.

I finish the fitting. Ms. Sharaff constantly asks me if I feel good in the wardrobe she has picked, and I do. She goes through racks and racks for wardrobe and picks a dress in a gray blue tone that I didn't think I would like the color of, but she is right again—this is a great color on me. I am in envy of her eye. I think all the clothing is perfect for the character of Carol Ann. Frank Yablans comes by with his assistant, Ilene. He is very exuberant and happy, too.

Lunch at Oblatt's. Meet Ed, the cameraman, there at the counter. He packs a gun and tells me to be careful with the crime wave. What crime wave? He just stresses to get and pack a gun, too. Yikes.

Rush back to bring tax form over to Mauri. Had forgotten to do so. Was taking short nap when Richard called: He and Kukums are arriving tomorrow at 8:30 p.m. It's funny how I want to see my cat more than my husband.

Wednesday, January 14th

I drive downtown to Bullock's to pick up a bathrobe for Richard. Go to bank for cash, get coffee, gas. Buy flowers for Richard—I don't know why. He should be buying flowers for me, but as long as he's here I just want peace and harmony for my life and my work. Call Michael, the A.D. (assistant director), regarding keeping Friday clear for the dentist. My tooth is really bothering me and it's the soonest my dentist can see me. Michael says we were scheduled for rehearsal at 3 p.m. I say I'll be a little late as I had to make sure that I wasn't going to have a dental problem when we were shooting.

I pick up Richard and Kukums and take them to the Chateau Marmont. Kukums wet his carrier box. We wipe his belly and tail with napkins and Kleenexes, then wash and towel him dry. He purrs so appreciatively, he is fastidious about cleanliness. After settling, we go to bed around 12:30 a.m. Richard is wiped out, he just wants to watch T.V. "Looks like a good movie," but I go to bed. I have to ask him to keep the volume down several times.

I miss my peaceful evenings of living with just the script.
I miss living with Joan Crawford as Carol Ann.
Ah, I feel a disturbance has come into my life.

Thursday, January 15th

I get up at 6:30 a.m. Set call is 7:30. Kukums was up all night playing and knocking things off the dresser, keeping me up. He is fascinated with watching the birds this morning. I put a chair by the window so he can watch from a comfortable vantage.

Get to the studio, do hair and makeup for younger Carol Ann. We are actually doing screen tests, which is not done anymore. The old stars used to do it regularly, so they and the director and cinematographer and everyone involved could see how the actress looks on film. This is such a thrill for me. I had never experienced this kind of luxury.

We prepare my character of Carol Ann for her first scene. Frank Perry comes in with Frank Yablans and says that I am pretty. I blush. He also says that Joan would not pick me up and hire me if I looked that pretty. Frank P. says that he thinks I am a fabulously good looking woman (wow) with great bones and great eyes. He also says I must not look this good and goes. We tone the makeup down a lot.

Frank returns after a while and tells me and the makeup man I still have to look plainer, less attractive. Frank says that he wants Carol Ann to be someone who blends in and never stands out, that if she stood out, Joan would have gotten rid of her (which is funny, because I had read and seen photos of how Joan surrounded herself with stylish and attractive people, like Betty Barker, Joan's real long-term personal secretary, who was as loyal but also appeared more independent and dignified than Carol Ann). He goes off.

Later, Frank comes back a third time and tells me and the makeup man that I still look too good. He seems a little frustrated now—embarrassed. Frank says if I look this good, Faye will have me fired and there is nothing that he, Frank, will be able to do about it. He is very adamant. So, I tell Charlie, look, I don't want to get fired, just make me look bad—bad's good. I get really sallow makeup and heavier brows, and he even makes little tips to add to the length of my nose. I look bad. That's good.

I go to Studio One and I am the first person who gets film-tested. Frank makes it easy with his constant sensitivity and reassurances to me and the cast. Michael Daves, the A.D., who incidentally was one of the children along with his sister at Cristina Crawford's actual birthday party, has brought photos of himself and the real Christina. Michael turns the chair so I get filmed 360 degrees. Michael tells me that Christina was not actually allowed to attend her own party, that she had to watch from the upstairs window, which is different from our script. I wonder what Joan had punished her for as they change the lens and do a close up at 360 degrees.

Then I go and change into the first age-change, the touch-of-gray hairpiece and slight age makeup. It looks really good. Frank likes it. The still man (charged with taking production photos of everything and everyone for continuity and posterity) doesn't recognize me. That's a good sign. Meet Erik, the wardrobe person for the men, and talk to him. He's German. He did the men's wardrobe for *The Deer Hunter*, but he also didn't recognize me. That's really good. I feel great about that since he knew me for six weeks on that shoot.

Faye is causing havoc. She isn't ready for her test, even by noon. Vivienne Walker, hair and wigs, was upset.

"Fuck her," she says.

I learn Faye keeps rejecting the beautiful wigs she had created for her and screaming criticism. The poor woman has been terrified for two days. Moreover, Faye's been in since 7:30 a.m. working on her hair with her own personal stylist. They came and got a stand-up salon dryer for her. I can't believe Faye has rejected the great Vivienne Walker, who worked on the real Joan Crawford among other legendary stars, and brought in Kathy Blondell, who did Goldie Hawn's hair in *Private Benjamin*. Apparently, Faye had loved Goldie's hairdo, but Vivienne says this is a period film and Joan cannot look like Goldie in the '80s. Furthermore, Vivienne says Kathy doesn't know how to do wigs, which is causing a real problem, as she keeps winding up doing the wigs for Kathy, which is not her job anymore—Vivienne is just doing the other female leads now. At best, this will be a lot of additional and uncredited work for her. Strains are developing, or maybe just starting to show.

I hear from someone in production that Anne Bancroft was originally offered the role of Joan Crawford, but turned it down. They said the money wasn't enough. They also said that Faye had heard about Bancroft and had made herself up like Joan, wore the period wardrobe, hired a vintage limousine, and drove to Frank Y.'s house and auditioned for him there.

(Frank Yablans' story is that Ms. Bancroft did want to play the part and was being considered for it by Frank. Terry O'Neill called him and said that Faye was very interested in playing Joan, and invited him to the set of *Evita* because she wanted to meet and talk with him, and he went and said you're a good actress, let me think about it. She asked to have dinner and he invited her to his house that Friday. Faye showed up in full hair and makeup in a Crawford type suit, looking just like Joan. He said that was it, and cast her right then and there. You can hear him tell it in his own words in the "Hollywood Royalty Edition" extras. Later, producer David Koontz confirmed the limousine element for me. For what it's worth, I've also heard a rumor that Ms. Bancroft also was seen at a back pain specialist at the time, lying immobile in the waiting room across multiple chairs, which if known would have affected the casting decision.)

I meet Diana Scarwid, who plays the older Christina. She tells me she doesn't remember my downstairs neighbors in New York, Mark and Jana, who implored me to say hello. Well, so much for that. A reminder that people we think know us don't necessarily remember us at all. Depressing.

Steve Forrest is very outgoing and polite, but little Mara Hobel, playing young Christina, seems like an adult in miniature, a bleached blonde, forty-five-year-old dwarf: "Who is your agent? What else have you done?" She keeps grilling me to list more of my credits; it's frustrating to be challenged to a pissing contest by anyone, but especially by a nine-year-old.

I go home for an hour—not to get résumés to give to children, but to have lunch—and then go back for a wardrobe fitting with Arda and Betty, Irene's assistants. Finished at about 3 p.m. Then go up to production office to get official Paramount stationery for my Latvian and Russian artist friends I made while in the Soviet Union. They'll flip out just getting the stationery. They are so in love with the old American movies and anything to do with the studios. To see a piece of paper with Paramount Studios on it will be a thrill for them. Also get some for Popi ("Papa," my father), stuck in Riga. He cannot get a travel visa to anywhere, let alone come and visit me. The Soviet government is afraid of the real America that they would see if they let people travel here.

Also, I need to get my paycheck. It had already been picked up, so Mauri and I go to the mail room on the chance we could recoup it. We do, so I go to the bank and cash it. Faye also caused ripples at the production office—heard comments about her, none good.

Friday, January 16th

Went to see Dr. Chin for our appointments. I have to have a root canal redone because the idiot dentist in New York perforated the root, so he has to cut the root off halfway—an operation which I'll do after the film. At least I know what is causing the pain. Richard has an abscess and two root canals to do and also we have to schedule the dental appointment for him—products of big drugs and little drugs, heroin and sugar, as well as laziness.

Take longer than expected. Madly drive to Paramount and I rushed into rehearsal forty-five minutes late—I am really nervous and my heart is racing. They were on page twenty-six when I came in. I nervously take my reserved seat in the room and know to whom to apologize: I look directly at Faye first and mouth "I'm sorry." She mouths back, "It's okay."

I settle myself down and just take in all my anxiety. It doesn't kill me. I'm still alive. As I get further along in the reading, I start enjoying myself. The scenes sound really good. Faye is throwing herself into it. So is Mara. Steve Forrest is here and Diana Scarwid, as are Frank Perry, Frank Yablans, and Marshall, the script supervisor. We take five during which Faye tells Frank Perry he was a genius at casting. Frank says we are the "true nucleus" of the group and he feels the power of us.

Faye looks at my little lapis lazuli pendant around my neck that Richard had given me for my birthday and loves it, then shows me her lapis bracelet, which puts my little pendant to shame. The beautiful stones are as big as quarters, about eight in all, set in gold. I notice that she wears an engagement ring as well as a silver wedding ring when she introduces me to her fiancé during the break—I don't remember his name, but later learn it's Terry O'Neill. I make sure, although I am polite, that I don't stay with him too long, as I don't want any misinterpretations of anything. I turn all my attention right back to Faye.

(I remember searching her face for any sign of recollection of ever having met me. She greeted me as if I were a total stranger. Okay, I thought, this is a good thing. She and I will start fresh.)

We go back to our little room and finish the reading at 5:30 p.m. Frank Perry says we would rehearse again next Wednesday, Thursday, and Friday, 12 to 6 p.m. On Friday, he will bring in the day players (the people who only had one day of work in one scene). During the break, I make sure to apologize to Frank and Frank for being late. They say not to worry. Frank Yablans jokes it's okay, I'm only fired. Then he asks me if it's serious. I tell him what I will have to have. He says he knows all about it and it's not bad, that he'd had that exact procedure done. Faye yells out the name of her dentist and says he's the best. Now I can't remember his name.

After we finish at 5:30 p.m. I kiss Faye on the cheek and tell her how happy I am to be working with her. She says she is so pleased to have me. I have Marshall walk me to the film room, where they will have a screening of all the tests from the other day at 6 p.m. Diana Scarwid follows us and we start talking. I tell her I'm going to Oblatt's first to meet Richard. She says she'll come along. She seems different, more willing to get to know me. I wonder if she heard something about me.

We talk about her wanting to relocate herself back home in Savannah, Georgia. She's been out here five years, really concentrating on her career. She feels lonely out here. Her marriage of one year is breaking up. Her husband is a doctor from Brooklyn. After her success in *Inside Moves*, she went back to New York to see him and just felt really confused. She'd like to meet someone back home in Georgia and get married and have a lot of kids and a career, too. She thinks it's all possible. She doesn't want to wind up like Joan Crawford with nothing but the work.

I wait with her for Richard at Oblatt's, who is supposed to be there at 6. It's ten after. We leave to go to the screening. We're late. Everything has started. She sees herself and Mara briefly and the rest is all Dunaway. I missed seeing my test. I feel a little bad. I should know better than to wait for Richard. He is chronically late. I am pissed at myself. I sit on the floor and see the rest of the tests. Faye looks stunning. The makeup, the wigs, the clothes—so much like Crawford in certain shots.

I talk to Frank Perry about my second makeup stage. The second A.D. had said to me that there was some question about it not being old enough. During one of Faye's tests, in which she wears a white cashmere coat, Frank Yablans says, "Oh, Irene, is it okay to have a two-hundred-and-eighty-five-thousand dollar pin on that coat?" Everyone laughs. Then Faye flips the lapel up near her face and Frank Y. says, "Oh, no lipstick all over the white coat!" Laughter. Afterward, Frank Y. and Faye seem pleased. Faye comments to Vivienne Walker that she takes it back about the wigs, they're fabulous and the shine is the best she's ever seen on any wig. She just has a question about the row of curls in the back. They agree they'll discuss it later.

I tell Irene Sharaff how wonderful the clothes are. She says, "Oh, there are forty-three more," but she seemed really pleased and her face lit up when I complimented her. She told me I looked great in the hair piece.

I stop to say goodbye to Faye before leaving. I tell her she looked fabulous. She tells me, "Oh, your face was so open and nice." Meet Richard at 7 p.m. He's sitting at Oblatt's. I go to the ladies room since I drank a Tab at the rehearsal out of sheer nerves. I never drink that shit. I don't mention that his lateness had caused me to miss myself in the screen tests, as I don't want any arguments.

We leave and go back to the Marmont. I play with Kukums. Get my mail and messages. Call Jane H., whose face got half-burned by scalding water at a facial salon. It was only a first degree burn and she got treatment from her homeopathic guy and is okay.

Fabulous dinner at Matoi, a Japanese restaurant. Too much,

really. I taste my first octopus and their horseradish makes us both cry and blows out our sinuses. It's shaped like a little green olive. But one tiny bite and oh, boy! We go back to the Marmont after a short walk.

I'm tired. I have to remember that I am still recovering from the flu. Can't wear down my body.

Saturday, January 17th

Go to Anna Marie's for a delicious dinner, after having studied the script again and again, then to Hollywood Boulevard to see *Scanners*, waiting in line thirty minutes, watching all the action on the Boulevard.

Sunday, January 18th

I take Kukums for a walk around the pool. He can't wait to get out for a walk every day. He still waits for me with the leash. Everyone thinks it's so strange to see a cat out for a walk. He loves to eat grass. We walk and sit for a while. Go shopping at Quinn's health food store for dinner. Make chicken at the Marmont.

Monday, January 19th

Wake up call 6:45 a.m. Have breakfast and Richard drives me to the studio. He comes in and says hello to Frank and Frank. More makeup testing. I redid makeup number two with bits of gray added to the wig. They wanted an older look. Faye comes in wearing a beautiful white dress with billowy sleeves. I introduce Richard. She leaves and comes in again soon after with another outfit.

More gossip back at the trailer with word that Faye is being very difficult with everyone, including Irene Sharaff. I got dismissed at 11:15 but hung around for a manicure with Helga at 2. I have decided that Carol Ann's nails have to be clean all the time. No polish, just really clean. Joan is obsessed with cleanliness and I have to be clean at all times. I finish at 2:30 and wait for Richard in my dressing room. Get tired around 4. Go to Oblatt's. Wait till 5. Get tired, call Richard at his agency. He's still there. Decide to take bus home as he has my car. Go to Melrose Avenue, get bus, and walk home from Crescent Heights. Kukums wants me hold him for the longest time. After our walk by the pool, Richard's back. We go eat at Bangkok, and on to Figeroa's for drinks and coffee.

Tuesday, January 20th

Pick up my personal photos of Christmas and Halloween from photo store. Back to Paramount for screening at 6 p.m. of test shots. The Carol Ann test shots look good. My middle-age makeup looks most effective. Frank and Frank not at screening. Faye is very upset about her wig being too red and she is letting everyone know about it. Go to King King Chinese restaurant for dinner, then buy Whisker Lickins for Kukums like I promised.

Watch the inauguration and Iranian hostage release story throughout the day.

Wednesday, January 21st

Wardrobe call 10:30 a.m. Got five more outfits. Ms. Sharaff has a wonderful eye. She says she ought to, she's been in the business a long time. I say I'd like to kidnap her for about two hours to take her shopping with me.

I have lunch at Oblatt's, then to rehearsal room at 1:00. No one there. Call hotel for messages. Rehearsal postponed till 2:30. Call Richard from production office. He'll meet me and have his lunch at Oblatt's. I wait and look through all the old photos in the book *Hollywood: The First 100 Years*. Good images for my imagination for this film.

Frank Perry comes in. I overhear his conversation from the other room. He says now they're negotiating as to who will replace him as a director if he dies during the shoot for insurance purposes. He just wants to get on with the film, says "Let the actors act and the directors direct." I sit on the couch outside. The assistant director and the production manager see me and wonder what I'm doing. I just say I'm thinking.

I meet Richard and he eats lunch. I just have a Perrier and lemon. He walks me to the rehearsal room. Frank Perry isn't there yet. We sit outside. Steve Forrest comes up and I introduce Richard to him. We talk about the Iran situation. Frank Perry comes up with Faye. Richard leaves and we go inside.

Frank takes Mara and Faye first—we now have half an hour. We go to stages eight and sixteen and see the sets. They are awesome and inspiring. (As former President of Paramount, Frank Yablans had access to many classic, treasured pieces of movie history, such as Pharaoh's throne from either DeMille's 1932 or '56 epic adaptation of *The Ten Commandments*, which time traveled to Crawford's dressing room and got a coat of white paint, as Roger Ebert later noted. It looked perfect.) As I walk around the sets I will work in, I imagine myself as having been there and having a life there. I walk around and around many times and touch the objects to get familiar with them and my imagination takes flight.

I come back to reality when Diana asks me what I think of Faye. I say I think she'll be fantastic in the role. She says Faye has driven Andrea, the wardrobe lady, into tears. Diana doesn't approve of that. I say nothing because I have to justify everything Joan does. Now, I also have the conflict in life that I have to justify everything Faye does. I have to be loyal to Faye as I am loyal to Joan. It is in straddling these two worlds that I will be challenged continually.

Diana says she has a lot of notes from Frank Perry on her character and she's scared. She wants to know if I get scared right before a show. Yes, I do. I say every actor probably does. I feel as though she's untrained. It seems like she has no technique for dealing with this. She must really be scared. I feel really bad for her.

Rehearsal goes very well. Frank is very pleased. I discuss my character with Frank. I mention that I think Carol Ann loves everything about Joan and she justifies everything Joan does. Joan is perfect in her eyes. I mention that if Joan discards her stockings, Carol Ann picks them up and caresses them and might even put them on her own legs later. If there is a drink that Joan has finished with her lipstick on it, Carol Ann might put her lips on that imprint on the glass. I mention my thoughts on putting away her underwear and caressing it, perhaps even caressing Joan when she is drunk. That if she undresses Joan when she's drunk, she does it in a tender way. Frank looks at me with a shocked look on his face. "Let's keep Carol Ann in the closet," he says. That's the end of that discussion. Well, he can't stop me from imagining it.

I ask for one line back that had been cut—he okays it. We get our blue pages (colored to show changes in the script). Meet Richard and go home and relax till 8 p.m., then meet David

Garfield and his wife, Sonja, for dinner. Afterward, they come and see our apartment at the Marmont and stay for a half-hour.

Oh, I have to take knitting lessons in Beverly Hills for a mutual activity to be shared with Faye. Joan was a big knitter. I take my knitting with me and practice every chance I get. Carol Ann and Joan share knitting. Joan was a big knitter and made many beautiful things. (I later learned Christina is an amazing knitter and makes great sweaters. I wonder if Joan taught her how.)

Thursday, January 22nd

Go to my knitting lesson at 11 a.m. at Darn Yarn in Beverly Hills. Learn two stitches and get more yarn to practice. Richard bought two shirts at Mr. Guys. He found me even though he'd dropped me off at the wrong address. I feel more and more Richard wants it to all be about him all the time. I need my time now for Carol Ann and I can't be just dropped off at the wrong address.

We go to Paramount to pick up my per diem check. Cash it at bank. Go back to Marmont for an afternoon nap. Rehearsal at 4. Faye is late. Frank Perry speaks to us all about how it wasn't Faye's fault. He says it's like F.D.R. said, "Everyone's nibbling a piece out of him." He says she had been at the studio since 6 a.m. for wardrobe fittings and then at the dentist this afternoon for teeth capping. Apparently she's recapping her upper and lowers. She had mentioned that she was going to recap her teeth for Joan, I just didn't think it was possible to do this all in a few days. With my dentist, capping is at least a three week process to do it right.

Frank P. relates a story of his dentist, how he went today and got his first laughing gas in Beverly Hills. The guy put stereo ear phones over his head and he was out for twenty minutes. Then, the dentist took off the ear phones and asked him who he thought was going to win the Super Bowl. Frank said, "Get out of here, you've got to be kidding." Frank also tells us to be careful, because two grips (crew members who construct, move, and maintain equipment that support cameras) were held up at gun point by two black women at the Van Ness gate entrance to Paramount. Maybe that guy was right about getting a gun—the conversation came back to my mind.

When Frank P. asks me and Steve Forrest to change seats, Steve says "Oh, thank you, what a warm seat," and Frank teases me. Frank says there are still contract problems with Faye that are not resolved. Also, he and Faye agree that we're always cursed when we are looking at ourselves—we're standing outside and watching no matter what we do. Frank says although rehearsal is fine and going well it shouldn't be at the expense of the performance on camera.

Faye comes in and Frank and Faye have a talk privately then join up with us. As it turns out, Faye didn't have the time to recap her teeth. We read just the blue page changes plus my first scene.

Mara made some pictures of mountains for Faye and asks me how to spell "sweet" and "Faye." I practice my knitting—told Frank he may get a muffler out of this. He was wearing a light purple sweater and checked shirt underneath. I'm thinking of colors for his muffler. Richard said that the salesman at Mr. Guy had said that Frank shops there and they are looking for bow ties for him, the George Cukor look.

Frank talks to Diana privately after rehearsal and I go to Oblatt's for a Perrier and lemon. At 7 p.m. go to Theater 8 at Paramount for screenings of *Mildred Pierce* (1945) and *Humoresque* (1946), two movies that star the real Joan Crawford. *Mildred Pierce* is fascinating and stylishly done. They bring deli food for us—I have a roast beef sandwich with pickles and coleslaw. Frank laughs through *Mildred Pierce*, as do I on certain lines. He says that we've lost something in American film. We watch part of *Humoresque*, but then the projectionist has a problem and we break.

I can't reach Richard so Diana and Rickie, her brother, give me a lift home. I watch the ABC report on all the hostage dealings. Go to bed at 1:30 a.m. Richard calls me saying he was having a good time with the guys and would be home late. He comes in at 7 a.m. I am mad. I am also suspicious. Drugs are now back in the picture. I am about to re-enter hell. Why had I told him to come?

Friday, January 23rd

(No entry.)

Saturday, January 24th

Stereo shopping. Richard wants a stereo. At this point I just want to get him comfortable so that he will stay off drugs and I can concentrate on my work. We really don't need a stereo system. We get an expensive one.

At Gita's for lasagna dinner. I bring the wine. Mark, a student I had auditioned for a while back for a University of Southern California student film (and not gotten the part), was there too. That's okay, it's preferable to work on a Paramount picture, given the opportunity.

Sunday, January 25th

I re-read the script once again. Take Kukums for a walk around the pool. We always get admired, or rather Kukums does. Meet the English couple next door. Paul Jenkins came over and we all went to Billy Devane's house for the Super Bowl and a chili dinner.

Monday, January 26th

Take Richard to Dr. Chin—root canal appointment. I have my second fitting with Ms. Sharaff at Paramount. She says that she's enjoyed doing me more than the star. At one point she asks the assistant "Is Faye behaving herself?" She also mentions talking to her doctor friend, a woman, about the complete indifference Faye has shown her. Her doctor friend said not to take it personally. Ms. Sharaff is concerned with my liking everything, which I do. This pleases her very much. The '50s gray taffeta dress is by a famous French designer and is for Joan's wedding scene. And my hat at the end is to be shades of Crawford at her funeral. (I don't know what that means, but I wrote it.) We also talked about how wonderful it is that I'm an actress, to put all the background of my life into a healing force. Betty, her assistant, mentions she was adopted but had good parents and was happy.

Meet Richard at Oblatt's—Gene and Marilyn, our friends, were there. Richard had brought them over. We talk for a while, then Richard goes over to join Paramount's gym, which he can do while I am working here.

Tuesday, January 27th

Go to the credit union to withdraw a thousand dollars to buy our first ever hi-fi set. I don't want to spend that much money as I'm not making a lot, but Richard insisted and persisted. With

Richard's explosive drug problem, if this will help keep him happy then I will do it.

I have a photo session with Buddy Jacobson for my personal head shot, paid for by me, during which I put on a Ronald Reagan mask to get a laugh.

Back home, Richard spends the whole evening just reading all the Technics hi-fi literature. I admit it is a wonderful mini-micro unit with great sound.

Wednesday, January 28th

Richard goes to unemployment and I go to knitting lessons, after which I reread my script. Dinner at Matoi with Barbara Clamen, a casting director. Back to her house discussing the industry and episodic T.V. Barbara reads poetry and Mae West.

Home at 2 a.m. I got pissed off at Richard because he wouldn't leave earlier, as this is too late for me, but he said he sensed a loneliness with Barbara. Why do I always come last in his priorities? He set a date for Friday for Michael McClure's poetry reading.

(Michael wrote "The Beard" in 1965, a very controversial play, in which Richard starred as Billy the Kid, playing in San Francisco, New York, Paris, and London. Richard was repeatedly arrested in California for performing "lewd and dissolute conduct in a public place" for cursing and simulating oral sex, though in today's world this play would seem tame. The American Civil Liberties Union helped fight the resulting court cases and uncensor our theatres.)

Thursday, January 29th

Call at 8:30 a.m. for stand-by shoot for scene fifty-two. I'm tired and I am pissed at Richard because he put someone else ahead of my work. Richard gets a call to go to Dr. Chin, so I am about to take a cab to Paramount, but a call comes: They won't need me until tomorrow's M.G.M. fan scene, when I first meet Joan as a fan that she has gotten to know through the years.

Go to Paramount to pick up my per diem check. Not there. Get a ride home. Richard is back with a bad headache. I wonder what he's taken to get that?

Friday, January 30th

Pick up the per diem check that wasn't there yesterday. Office is having lunch catered and so Richard and I have some. Found out that Neil, the production manager, had worked on *The Panic in Needle Park* (1971), a film in which Richard was one of the stars and I had a small part. Neil recognizes Richard, which makes Richard happy, as he has a need to be recognized. His ego needs that constant attention.

Go to bank and cashed check. Give Richard the money. Why did I do that? Why am I feeling guilty for working and then giving him my money? I have a deep problem here. I don't want to support him anymore. He spends all his money on drugs and I wind up picking up all the bills for us both. I can feel the weight of him. I feel trapped and don't have the guts to leave. A woman in a trap—that's me. There has to be a way out. I am not brave enough now.

Pick up proof photos at Buddy Rosenberg's. Rush back to the Marmont for Michael McClure's scheduled phone call—just missed it. McClure calls again at 5:15 to meet in Venice for dinner. We get lost on the way, but meet him and have dinner at Siamese Gardens, then off to a bookstore for his poetry reading. The night is a success for Michael—full house with people standing in the back. Lasts about one hour. Go to a café on the beach afterward, then take Michael and his wife Joanna back to the Marmont. I drive the car with Joanna and Michael goes with Richard. Management puts a roll-away cot in our living room for them to stay the night.

Saturday, January 31st

Joanna got up early for a conference in Pasadena. I met Richard and Michael at Schwab's at 10:30 for breakfast. (Schwab's was a famous drug store and coffee shop where a lot of actors hung out there and Lana Turner was rumored to have been discovered. I once had lunch at the counter and Jerry Brown, who was then the young governor of California, sat right next to me without any bodyguards and we chatted like we knew each other. It was that kind of place.) Back to the Marmont and run into the wonderful actress, Cathleen Nesbitt. She looks fabulous at ninety-two.

Go for a walk down the Strip with Richard and Michael. Come

back and Michael gives us an autographed book. He had a very bad toothache from the Orbit gum I had given him—I'm glad he didn't yell at me. Joanna comes back. I study my scenes again and take a one hour nap. We dine at Matoi, then say our goodbyes.

Richard and I go see "Julius Caesar" with Paul Jenkins in it. Terrible. Go out with the cast afterward at Theodore's. Bad vibes. Richard told one of the actors he didn't like the play after the guy made the mistake of asking him. Reminder to never ask unless you really want to know. Most people don't want to.

Sunday, February 1st

Got call sheet for work on Monday, call time 7:30 a.m. Went to have pancakes at Du-par's for a late breakfast. They have the best pancakes and I need something sweet right now in my life. Go to a play reading of our friend Don Blakely (who in 1983 starred in *Vigilante* with me and Richard), then afterward to another friend Caesar's house. Don Gerler, Richard's agent, is there. Caesar is showing his son's clippings and ads—he is mentoring and pushing his young son into show-business. I have mixed feelings about this, as it is such a hard business, and even harder on children.

Came home early to a message: Bob, the assistant director, telephoned to cancel my call—said they'd be shooting at the studio on Monday (we were supposed to be on location at M.G.M., I think). I get a little worried I have a terrible pang in my chest that all of a sudden that something may have gone wrong. Richard says I was silly and not to worry, it has nothing to do with me. Still, I don't have a good feeling and I can't seem to shake it. What is going on? Am I going to be fired? My heart and brain are racing. I feel helpless. There is nothing that I can do.

I learn that the entire production is on hold. Word is out that unless Faye's boyfriend, Terry O'Neill, gets producer credit, Faye is not going to do the part. I hear Frank Yablans is furious and feels he's being blackmailed. Duuhhh. There has been so much money invested in sets, bespoke and vintage clothing, hiring actors and crew, but the film could still be stopped. This is a tense time. I am on pins and needles with anxiety.

Finally, I get word that the film is on—Faye has won, and Terry will get credit in spite of not doing any producing.

Monday, February 2nd

Walk down Hollywood Boulevard and stop at Grauman's Chinese Theater to look at the hand- and foot-prints in the cement. Wow! There are Joan's. I put my hands into her hands in the cement. They fit, and I get shivers that go all through my body. I withdraw my hands quickly. Oh boy. Is this a sign of chilling things to come?

I shake it off and go pick up Richard's photos, then to Dr. Foster, a chiropractor, for an adjustment: turns out I had a pinched nerve.

Later at home, I feel I have to write Elia Kazan a letter. I often write him. His wife, Barbara Loden, was my dear friend and acting teacher and she directed me in her workshop production of a lost-and-found Eugene O'Neill play that we were in rehearsal to perform, when she died suddenly of breast cancer September 5th of last year. I still dream about her at night—her passing has left an empty spot in my heart and my gut. I miss her terribly. I miss my best friend and I hear her voice in my head when I read my part and study the script over and over again.

Dear Elia,
I've been writing a letter in my head to you many times—so let me try it on paper. I'm out here working on Mommie Dearest, *a job that came suddenly and inexplicably but is a blessing. I've been working by myself on my scenes and I start my first day tomorrow.*

I think of Barbara so many times. I hear her voice so clearly in my head. I'll forever be grateful to her for the help and support she gave me and what she taught me. Even now while working on my scenes—I hear her. I'll just try so hard to live up to what she gave me and also what she awakened in me as to my own potential. Sometimes I get so scared and I can hear Barbara say "Come on Rutanya, you can do it—just do it." She was so courageous. I just love her so. As long as I live, she'll always be a part of me. She was responsible for so many major changes in me.

I'm sorry I didn't get to stay for all of Wanda *(Barbara's wonderful 1970 film in which she starred and directed) at the public memorial.* (We had the private memorial service from a shortlist that Barbara had prepared before she died of people she loved and wanted at the house. I made it after driving nonstop from Salinas, Kansas, to New York to be there. Barbara specified in her will that she did not want her service held at the Actors Studio, which Kazan supported as he had already disassociated himself from them.) *I remember sitting quietly at the wooden kitchen table with you. Neither one of us said very much. Later, at the public memorial, I had to leave early because I was acting in a play at St. Clement's Theater and barely made curtain. Richard said he saw you afterward and spoke with you briefly. I saw you sitting in the back row right before the lights went out, but you looked so very private. I didn't want to—I mean I wanted to—but yet I couldn't intrude. I'll never forget the way you sat there in your green sweater.*

Anyway, I just wanted to touch base. I'll be working here till April sometime. I will see you when I get back. I play Joan Crawford's secretary. Faye Dunaway plays Crawford.

With love,

Rutanya

P.S. Elia, I would like to have a photo of Barbara. We were supposed to take pictures last spring with my camera, but never got around to it. I didn't realize time was so fleeting. However, if it would upset you in any way, please forgive me and just believe it comes from my heart. (Elia was a sensitive man. I remember working on his last film, *The Last Tycoon*, which we shot at Paramount in 1976. At the wrap party, Elia came up and told me, "Just get out of here, Hollywood is a terrible place to be.")

Tuesday, February 3rd

On "will notify" for work. Waiting for the phone to ring. Mauri calls to let me know that (associate producer) Neil Machlis' three-year-old son died yesterday and the funeral is today. How absolutely awful. I get another call at 1:30 p.m. to come in, so we go to Schwab's to get a sympathy card.

Go to check in on the set—Michael Daves, the assistant director, says it will be a while. Frank Perry is not open to seeing me—a lot on his mind. I catch myself and say "it's not personal" after he walks by without even acknowledging me. It's just that I feel so insecure when things like that happen, so I just have to talk to myself a lot.

    I check into my dressing room and go to makeup and hair. Hair first. Vivienne says how well today was going compared to last week. Faye has changed all the wigs—cut them, in fact. Diana is there for a hair and makeup test. Go to look for Charlie Schram and run into Leo, who saw my play "And They Put Handcuffs on the Flowers." (I directed the West Coast production and also acted in it. It was an incredible run and I received love letter reviews from *The Los Angeles Times* and *The Herald-Examiner*).

    In makeup, Charlie does my face and tells me last week was a disaster—they almost didn't think the show would go on. Faye had kept everyone waiting six or seven hours before even coming on the set. She had changed her makeup from the tests we had done. She had ordered Paul, the director of photography (D.P.), to change the lighting, and more.

    I go over to Paul and he gives me his chair to sit in. It doesn't take long for Jeremy, the baby Christopher, to become distracted and start looking around, leading Faye to wave wildly in my direction and yell "Clear, clear!" I scoot. Paul is the only one who sits, reading *The Wall Street Journal*.

    Charlie comes over, "Welcome to the Clear Away Club."

    "Are there other members in the club?"

    "We all are members—Faye is the President and clears us all away," he says. Last week on the beach, apparently, they all got cleared away behind the boom mic (quite the logistical feat, to hide a dozen people behind a man holding a slender pole). Charlie says if an actress can't stand people looking at her, she shouldn't act.

    Irene Sharaff comes in and wants to see my dressing gown, so we walk to my dressing room. She tells me I won't get to my scene today, but she doesn't want to be the one who tells me officially. We check the gown. I tell her how wonderfully thin she is, and she says it's because she eats right and doesn't drink anymore—she can't drink after having had hepatitis. She tried once, and it made her sick for hours. I tell her how much we all like her. She says she likes everyone, except Faye. She's never worked with anyone as crazy in all her years in the business. She tells me Faye is on drugs, that's why her behavior is so erratic. I ask cocaine? She says she doesn't know but believes that a couple of years ago it was heroin. She says her behavior is completely instant gratification—she wants it now, right away, like an infant. She's never seen anything like it. She says everyone hates her so much—they're just waiting for her to fall on her face so they can all laugh at her. I thank her for telling me so that I'm aware of it. She says don't cry in front of her—that's what she wants. I walk Irene over to wardrobe, then go back to the set.

Faye does not acknowledge me at all, all afternoon. Each time she comes from her dressing room, she walks in a huff straight for the set, not acknowledging anyone. I decide the best way to get along on this is going to be by hiding until needed.

I read the paper and then talk to Steve Forrest. He's genuinely happy to see me. I get the word about 5:30 that I won't work. Ms. Sharaff was right. Frank Perry finally comes up to me and says he's sorry—"It's been really rough, really rough." I say it's because you have to be with it every moment. He asks how Richard is and I say "Fine." I'm lying through my teeth, I wonder if he knows it. Frank asks how is my knitting really coming along. I tell him his scarf is about three feet long—"Good, good." His eyes are warm again. I say goodbye to everyone and get a will-notify for tomorrow.

I go up to Neil's office to give my personal condolences—they say he won't be back until tomorrow. I make sure he'll get my card. I feel so bad for him about the death of his little boy.

I wait for Richard at Oblatt's. He picks me up with Paul Jenkins. Not a good sign. We call Sam Peckinpah to see if he can join us for dinner. He's got diarrhea. We go to dinner at Ho Sai Gai and talk about a lot of things. Paul mentions what a shit Ralph Waite is and how he once beat up Paul's four-year-old son, when Waite was living with Paul's ex-wife.

(I have my own memories of Ralph beginning in New York, when I was a waitress and he was out of work and used to come in because I would give him free hamburgers. When I was in L.A several years later, I had a desperate situation where I needed money for rent that month. By then, he was one of the stars on *The Waltons*, a hit T.V. show, and he was making really good money. He was no longer an out of work actor. He offered to lend me the $200 I needed for rent. I told him I needed a job, not a loan, but he wouldn't even introduce me to the casting director. I took the $200 and then he told me the following week he wanted the money back. I gave it back to him.)

Wednesday, February 4th

On "will notify." Reread script and my scenes. Richard's lent Paul Jenkins three hundred of my dollars. I know we'll never get it back. I am pissed.

Take Kukums for daily walk around the pool—we save little Billy's life, a two-year-old English boy who falls in. There is no one else around, no parents watching. Richard hears me yell and jumps across some tables and we both bend over the deep end and grab his arms and hoist him up. He doesn't cry—he doesn't realize how serious this was. No, actually, he does start crying, because his green lollipop is still in the pool. Richard rescues his green lolly with the big pool scoop and he stops crying. His parents finally show up and we tell them what happened and they don't seem concerned at all. This should have at least quivered their stiff upper lip. Lucky for them we were there. Do they know that?

Thursday, February 5th

There is talk of an upcoming Screen Actors Guild strike. Ellen Whitman stopped by. She has gotten the stage manager job on "Coupla White Chicks Sitting Around Talking" 'cause she needs the money. Ellen is a former neighbor of mine in New York, she is smart and funny and I like her very much. Paul Jenkins also comes by. Not good news that he is around so much. Where there's Paul, there are drugs.

I go down to the pool to walk Kukums, then to Paramount at 2 p.m. for a manicure. Pick up per diem check, give it to Richard. Why am I doing this? I am totally insane. But if I don't, he will have a shit fit. Trying to maintain peace at any price.

Wait around all afternoon.

They get me in hair and makeup at 5 p.m. Vivienne says there only four awful people she's ever worked with on movies: Liza Minnelli, Barbara Streisand, Lauren Bacall, and Faye Dunaway. Faye walks in briefly, fortunately not at that moment, and I say "Hi, Faye," she says "Hi, Rutanya," and that's that.

Charlie shows me my life mask and age appliances that I would get later on my face for the old age part. Charlie tells us that he had done the makeup on Judy Garland when she died for her funeral. He didn't want to, but Liza and her husband had begged him with tears in their eyes. He had made Judy up as a child and it was very emotional for him. The conventional makeup did not stick and they had to use a kind with a lot of glue in it. He said her face's skin color was almost as black as my pants. "People who die from barbiturates turn dark," and apparently he had a hell of a time recreating her tones, it took about two hours. Listening to the story, Vivienne takes a slug of Maalox. To top it off, Jan, Vivienne's assistant, says she hopes her husband never comes back from location because she's divorcing him.

For dinner, Richard meets me at Oblatt's. I'm sitting with David Koontz, who is one of the producers, as well as the husband of Christina Crawford. Richard is mad I am not waiting out front, et cetera—I'm the one with the job, you should be waiting for me.

Oh, earlier on the set Frank Perry came up to me and told me I had the most beautiful eyes.

I said, "No, you."

He said, "No, you."

Frank Yablans said, "Oh, they're okay." Then Michael Daves, the first A.D., said the rushes were fantastic. Michael mentioned that he had been at the real Christina's birthday party as a kid and remembers that Christina was not allowed to come to the party, and just looked down at all the kids having fun from a second story window. He had told us this story before.

Friday, February 6th

Nervous as hell. Got only about four or five hours of sleep. Woke up at 6 a.m. for a 7 a.m. call. My car got blocked in by four other cars in the parking garage, so I am about ten minutes late. I had also run into Nicholas Colasanto. (I had met Nicholas in New York when he was an actor. He went to Hollywood, became a television director, and then later went back into acting when he got a job as a regular on *Cheers* as Coach. Nicholas was always amazed that I did so many odd jobs in New York to support myself—he told me I could make more money being a hooker.) I hate to be late, I get so anxious. Turns out to be no matter.

Go to hair. Doesn't turn out too well the first time, so Vivienne redoes it into Marcel waves. Charlie gives me a slight grayish base and adds an extension to my nose, which gives me a worse look. I look very plain. That's good.

Shoot my first scene—my big scene with little Christina. Finally. I feel it went well. I look at Frank. Frank has tears run down his cheeks. He says it was sensational. He says it was the first truthful scene of the movie. I am a little taken aback by that. How can that be? They've shot with Faye for days.

Frank is very supportive on the set. After the master shot, I want to do one more take. "Save it for the close-up," he says. "That's where the money is." After the close up, tears well up again in Franks eyes. I am willing to do one more but he said no, he had it, couldn't be better.

Have lunch on set. Richard came by—I had a feeling he would at that time. Earlier, a crew member told me he thought I was a very sexy woman. Uh oh, I thought.

"I'm supposed to be Ms. Plain."

"You think a hair-do is what it means to be sexy?" I told him I didn't know what that meant, but really I was terribly flattered by him and didn't know how to react. The fact that another man thought I was sexy and desirable awakened me in a deep way. It had been a long time since a man had told me that. I was deeply moved, so I tell Richard, and he gets mad and wants me to show him who said it—I won't. I say it was meant as a compliment, not derogatorily. Why did I tell Richard? I think it was because my own husband doesn't look at me like that anymore. His drugs are his mistress and his love.

I will shoot the second scene of mine with Faye in the afternoon, the Veda-Mildred Pierce scene. She has me come to her room on the next stage to listen to the original Veda tape from the film. I feel it doesn't help me because I'm not trying to be Ann Blythe, the actress—since Carol Ann is not an actress, she shouldn't be that good. But I don't say anything and I thank her. She also rehearses it with me and Frank before break, and then keeps everyone waiting an hour after lunch.

Frank Yablans comes by and sits down behind me and starts

talking to Frank Perry. Frank P. says she'll be here when she gets here. Frank Y. says he's feeling depressed today. I say why, is it a new moon? He says no—it's because the executives at Paramount hadn't bugged him for two weeks and he was feeling neglected. Frank P. says we can take care of that, we'll have them give you a call. I tell Frank Y. to forget the two-hundred-and-eighty-five-thousand dollar pin that Faye was wearing, I'd take the Lincoln convertible that I will be driving for a scene later instead. He laughs and says at least it's good that I don't want the pin. I say at least I want a Polaroid picture of me in the car. He says I can have a regular picture and if that's all I want I won't have any trouble at all.

Faye finally comes. She's very concerned every minute with her hair and makeup—she is full of nervous energy, but also seems very strong. We rehearse and start shooting. I tell her if there's anything she wants to do, if I can help her in any way, I would. I think she appreciated that. What I was saying is you're the star here and I'm not out to do you in or steal your scenes.

In the master shot, she stages the scene to upstage me so that my face would be away from the camera. I recognize the classic trick and think to myself, to whom am I going to complain? Frank Perry, as much as he likes me, would have to side with Faye no matter what. So, I decide right then and there that I will help Faye. I will help her upstage and block me. I go along with it. I upstage myself at every opportunity. I don't fight it at all. That's what Carol Ann would do. I felt that she relaxed with me doing that. I'm not going to compete with her. Instead, I am going to help her, and in so doing, I am going to help myself!

Frank asks me to really "act" Veda, not to do it so normally, so I do. Then Faye asks me on her close-up to look down when she slaps me. I do. I am squeezed in a very tight space by the camera operator. Then, Frank and Faye ask me to read Veda normally. I do.

It is late. Mara has already wrapped. They got a quick close-up of her. I'm concerned that they won't have time for my close-up. Faye keeps not being satisfied—she thought she got it on the third take, so did Frank P., but she did about seven or eight takes nonetheless. One of them I really got slapped hard. Oh boy! Red finger marks still on my face.

Finally we get to my close-ups, which I really appreciate. Right before, I eat a little Hershey bar and guess who comes in as I am about to put it in my mouth? Caught again. Richard is so critical of me when I eat chocolate or do anything without his approval. He's afraid I'll get fat. Frank P. sees Richard and comes over and very kindly tells him that this is the best day of shooting and that he got the best scene yet on film today with me. Richard asks why is that? Frank P. says because she's talented and it was real. I didn't know what to say. We finish at 7:52 p.m., almost twelve hours later. I am feeling tired, but Faye wants me to stay for all her close-ups right by the camera—she says that it really helps her to look at me. Of course I'll stay. Faye does not stay for my close-ups. I do them with the script person.

Afterward, I go to change. There is a cast and crew food and drinks party on the stage. Talk to Frank Y.—he says we go back to *Greetings* (1968). He's never forgotten me and I'm his good luck charm. I say you bet and if you're afraid of the upcoming Friday the 13th, come to me because that's my good luck day. He says he's not superstitious. He says he spoke to Frank P. about me and it was he who said Frank P. had to see me in New York. He says Frank P. called him back the next day and said, "Oh, yeah!" I say I didn't know it came from you and gave him a hug. Richard and I leave after a few more minutes, cued by Ileen Maisel (Frank Yablans' assistant) doing impressions of Faye screaming, "Clear the set!" Faye had cleared everyone away again on her close-ups earlier after someone's movements had distracted her. I was afraid to be associated with it and wanted to leave (though I did find it funny). I was afraid of Faye's reaction if she heard about it and heard I was there—Terry O'Neill, Faye's fiancé, had said to us that Faye was quite fond of me.

We head home and relax. Paul Jenkins phones and comes by after 11 p.m. and stays until 1 a.m. with some new girlfriend. Richard and I stay up and talk and listen to music on the hi-fi till 3 a.m. Go to bed exhausted.

Saturday, February 7th

Read the script again and my scenes. Do errands in the

afternoon. Go down to the Grand Olympic Auditorium for the boxing fight, mobs of people, around 6,000, drunk and pushing to get in. Richard and I get separated when I go to park the car and he to pick up our tickets. I'm swept up in the mob for a short time, with the police with billy sticks pushing and whacking to get them out of the street. I get scared and know this is no good and go across the street hoping Richard would find me. He does after a few anxious moments during which I thought about standing on the roof of a car.

"Let's get out of here," he says. There was no way to get through, even for our tickets.

We drive to Little Tokyo to get the acupuncturist's name—Dr. Nagatani—and then to the Atomic Cafe, where the punk Japanese waitresses and other punkers are. We play the jukebox.

Come back home and change to go to Bo Hopkins' party at the Continental Hyatt House. We greet Bo first and then wander around. See Pat Harris, R.G Armstrong, Ed Begley, Penny Marshall, and Cindy Williams. Ed says, "Cindy, have you met Rutanya?" She says no, but I had met her several times, so I tell her and am curt with Cindy. I had lost Richard and was pissed. It's uncomfortable being there without him with all the drunks. Find him. We do a square dance number together that's fun with a group of people, and then a slow dance. They introduce all the cast of *Dynasty* like some game show. Paul Jenkins is here, drunk. Run into Vincent Mongol, who has now changed his name to Aaron something. Vincent was responsible for telling me about the *Greetings* audition for Brian De Palma a few years prior, and I am eternally grateful to him.

Richard and I walk home and my feet kill me in the high heels. We do look elegant though, both of us.

Sunday, February 8th

I sleep till 11 a.m. Don't go fishing. Rains all day. Richard makes phone calls and goes to Joe Allen's restaurant to meet Paul J.—not good news. I stay in. I have an early call tomorrow at the studio, they've changed the scenes because of the forecast.

Monday, February 9th

Arrive at makeup 7:10 a.m. Really raining this morning. There were a lot of cars skidding on Sunset Boulevard, including mine. This Mustang really skids, and it was scary. I almost hit someone. Head to the dressing room to wait—they weren't ready for me.

I am mad at Richard. He didn't get in till 1:30 a.m. last night. He was with Paul and friends at Joe Allen's. I was worried because he was so late and he didn't call. He had three cappuccinos and couldn't sleep, so he kept me up. I feel he's not honoring my work and my schedule. He could be more helpful as I have a full day ahead of me.

I lie down in the dressing room from about 10 to 11:30. I fall asleep, dreams come to me and I could also hear people talking, cars, and radios. It was most refreshing. I awake and go to check where we are in the shooting. I am told I will be an off camera voice for Faye's scene, instead of being on camera. Faye wants the camera to be on her the whole time. I am upset and even more so when Frank has me stand behind the camera with my back toward Faye. I have to turn my back on everyone. It is a little like being the school dunce. I feel humiliated and fight to stay in control of myself. I understood immediately that Faye wants the scene all to herself and obviously my face or expressions now interfere with her preconceived way that the speech or scene should go. I tell myself to let go of it—it isn't worth it. I'll take my camera time when I can in the very few scenes without Faye.

I go to my trailer afterward and silently scream and make my hornet eyes and raise my hands up and hit down, still silently screaming I hate you, I hate you. I feel relief. Go to get a newspaper. Funny: My horoscope says to be a humanitarian or learn to be one today. I wait till about 4 p.m. Call Richard at 3:30 to leave message. I finish knitting the yarn I had with me, the scarves are coming along.

I rehearse scene sixty-two, waking up the kids. I gave little Jeremy, who plays Christopher, a warm look and hug and he responded immediately. What a wonderful little boy. Mara is very loving—I give her plenty of hugs, rub her little back. She loves it.

Frank Y. takes me around the back of the set to walk on the white carpet stairway and talk about fear and Joan's craziness—it's about being afraid for the kids. We shoot it three times. Last one is good, did a single shot on Mara. I put in a clap with my hands when I tried to wake up the kids. He liked it, told me to keep it in. Finished fast. Frank gives me a kiss on the way out.

Had run into Steve Forrest—he was talking about how the Russians will invade Poland, he thinks, and how if there is a war in the Mid East, as he thinks there might be, he would go immediately. He's in the Army Reserve and "strong as a bull." (He had fought at the Battle of the Bulge during the Second World War.) His three sons would go too, but that would worry him, because he's had his good life and they need theirs. Also, Vivienne bought me special shampoo and conditioner and gives them to me. I am touched. Call my agent, Kendall, regarding checks, they're ready tomorrow. Richard meets me on the set. I say goodbye to Terry and Faye on the way out.

Talk to Richard, have spaghetti dinner. Richard and Kukums take a nap. I hope I can sleep tonight.

Tuesday, February 10th

Report for makeup test for the really old age at 7 a.m. Wait around all day till 5:30 p.m. before they can fit me in. It took Charlie two hours to apply it and another half-hour for the wig. It looked amazing. We had to stop in between for Mara's makeup.

I was thinking that they could fit me in between scenes real quick for my photo test, but things have gotten real tense: It is the hair cutting scene with Faye and Mara. There are only three wigs available for Mara, so only three takes. They have to get it all in three takes. After the first, Mara's arms are all red from where Faye had grabbed her and Charlie has to cover them with makeup. The second take they get even more bruised when she grabs her so hard. More make up. On the third and final take, Faye somehow stabs Mara with the scissors, as well as giving her more bruises. Mara comes off the set crying, "She stabbed me, she stabbed me." They rush her to her dressing room behind the set. The welfare worker-teacher asks to see Mr. Perry (a welfare worker is mandatory on the set for minors, who, like with other licensed child labor, cannot work full days). Mara's mother is sitting there quietly. She knew what the scene entailed. Frank P. goes inside and closes the door. They are in there about five minutes. Afterward, Frank goes to Faye's dressing room, and Faye goes over to Mara's dressing room, and Frank breaks everyone for lunch—inserts will be done after (inserts are cutaway shots to the hands, scissors, somebody's expression, small detail things).

Frank Y. comes over and he and Frank P. talk. I only overhear him tell Frank Y. that Mara had been hurt and was upset. Things are smoothed out after lunch and Mara's bruises were touched up again. Of course, it helps that Faye or the company had bought and sent over several large stuffed animals and dolls. Apparently, the scissor puncture wasn't that deep and Mara told Charlie that whatever he had put on it, the doctor had said was fine and didn't touch it. I don't think little Mara, because of her young age, really understands what it means to be a physically abused child—she's had no such experience in her young life.

Things move on and around 4 p.m. they shoot me finally, after the other scene had been completed. I call Richard after but he isn't there. Again, the possibility of drugs flashes in my mind. It takes hot water and a steaming towel to remove the latex off my face, because we had to peel the application loose. Hurts like hell, especially around the neck, where it's left red welts. Richard came at 5:30 p.m. I ask Mauri to exchange my airline ticket for cash. She said she'd check into it. Went home to wash the gray off the top of my hair. In bed by 1:30 a.m.

Wednesday, February 11th

Up at 6 a.m., off to the studio. It takes about two hours to do the middle age make up and they cut the gray wig shorter upon my encouragement. Wait till after rehearsal with Faye. They do the handsome young jock scene and they fit me in around 12:30. Paul, the D.P., came in for a haircut while they were having a conference on the scene. Irene Sharaff is on set and showed me an article in the paper about our film and the troubles with Faye. She asks if Faye had given me a hard time yet. "Nothing I couldn't deal with," I say, and that I didn't show any emotion in front of Faye. She says that's the best way.

Frank P. comes over. Irene likes my makeup and hair and she asks Frank Y. if he's seen it. He says oh yeah and yesterday's makeup was even more startling. Frank P. is a little concerned about the dark spots in yesterday's scenes but hasn't seen the dailies yet. I show Irene a picture of Popi (my father), she says I look just like him. We talk about the possibility of his coming to America this year. Frank Y. introduces me to casting director Pam Dixon. He tells her my sweetness shows through even in old age. I say, it's because it is seen through your eyes, Frank.

They film my camera test and Charlie steams my face and peels me again. I ask Bob for a driver to take me home—don't want to take the bus with the half-gray head and the red skin, I look weird. John, a driver, takes me home.

Oh, I almost forgot: Vivienne told me how Mara had gotten more presents from Faye and a big Teddy from Frank and Frank to continue making up with her and have her feel good. Vivienne had said to me she thought we ought to stop at the gray wig and gray aging and not to go on to the really old age on me, and to tell Frank P. myself, and not to mention that she said it or she would deny it. I recall a moment from the day before, Frank Y. asked me did Faye see my makeup?

I said, "Oh yes, she did, and she liked it."

"I bet she did."

Also, when Faye had me back to act the scene the other day, I heard her in the room give a line reading on my line and how I should say it. The line was "I'm sorry, Joan." It was really emotional and Frank came back to tell me Carol Ann should be afraid. I didn't want to do my line the way Faye had done it, because when people are upset the other person very often tries to stay calm, even though they are upset, to calm them down, and Carol Ann would do that. I concentrated on really listening to Faye with my eyes and feeling afraid and letting those feeling determine how my line would come out. It even surprised me. I stuttered on can, can, can you go back to sleep. I knew Carol Ann's objective was to help her, to calm her down, to serve her—not to have a confrontation with her. If Carol Ann did that, she would have been fired by Joan. That much I knew, as I had worked very hard on my character.

Thursday, February 12th

Day off. Go to Aida Grey skin treatment place in Beverly Hills at 11:30 for treatment to try and bring down the redness and swelling from all the glue and appliances on my face. Off to the studio production office to pick up my check and leave the bill for the skin treatment. Stop by and visit with David Koontz. A big photo of Joan hangs in his office. He says it was Joan's favorite shot of herself. (That surprised me. It was an early picture of her—not really young, but probably from when she first came to the studio, before the big brows and lips. Her freckled face was very innocent and she had a three-quarter smile.)

Off to the bank to deposit my salary check. Go home for a while and then to visit Harrison Starr, Richard's friend, who was in the film business. He has a nice wild female cat of ten years of age. Exchange cat stories. Meet his wife, Sandy, an art historian.

Come home and am watching the news when we hear loud noises and people yelling. Richard goes to the window and says, "Please don't do that." The woman next door has her drapes out the window and is yelling at her friend that Kukums is going to jump—she is actually encouraging it. Richard shuts the window and we go back to sleep.

Friday, February 13th

Lucky Friday the thirteenth. Work call today is at 3 p.m. for wardrobe and makeup, then set call at 5 p.m. Richard drives me to M.G.M., where we will shoot the scene where Carol Ann is hired by Joan. We find the makeup trailer and he leaves. I finish makeup and hair and go to look for a Valentine's card—none to be found, go back to trailer and look over my scene. I have really justified "meeting" her many times before, but this is the first time she stops and talks to me, and I tell her that I will always be there to see her, that I will always be there for her. I am called for rehearsal, then sent for dinner break. Too bad, I was really prepared to shoot.

Caterers are inside gate and we eat in the commissary. Fish and salad. See Mauri and her husband, Paul, who is French, long-haired—a young drummer. Nice couple, been married for two-and-a-half years. I kid Mauri about how now I know why her French is so good. We sit down to eat with John, the driver from the previous day, then go dress. I had taken my wardrobe off, so in case of a food accident it wouldn't be on my clothes.

Finally, Bob comes and gets me for a rehearsal. Faye is in the car now instead of Victoria, her stand-in. (Production teams hire actors to literally stand in for the cast while crews prepare shots, saving time and money, as well as allowing the actors to save their energy and concentrate.) Lots of fan extras on set—one really obnoxious one asks if I helped beat up "the kid." I give him a cold look and turn my back on him. One really obnoxious aggressive girl gives me thirty questions until finally I say I don't want to talk about it. Her name is Wendy and she seems blind in one eye—her pupil is white. There is also a pretty blonde girl who first says she's studied with John Lehne, an acting teacher and friend of mine, for six months. Turns out, she is really studying with Reno, his assistant, whom I don't know.

We rehearse with Faye, then shoot the master, then the close-up of Faye. I give my very best. Frank's note to me is not to let myself get caught up in Faye's urgent rhythm. To maintain that, I've rehearsed this many times—I have my time now and I'll take it. By the time it came for my close-up it was about 11:30 p.m. and I had to forget about being tired.

My first take is good but I go out of the light by leaning in too much. Also, Wendy, the extra, leans her head into my close-up and blocks me. Her good eye works just fine—I wonder if the white one does too. I love what Faye does—she takes her prop pencil and moves the girl's head away with it, while signing autographs as Joan. I really admire her authoritative and immediate way of dealing with this girl. Wendy has gotten upgraded with one line, so she thinks that gives her permission to be pushy. I feel like elbowing her in the ribs, but I hesitate. I'm saying my dialogue and I'm wishing I had jabbed her. So, my second close-up wasn't as good, I feel—I am distracted by Wendy and myself. I tell Frank I didn't feel I was with it as much. He agrees, but says he's going to a wider angle, and we'd do it on that. The take on the wider angle is the best one yet. I thank Faye. She says she wants to add more lines on the jogging scene with us—to show that I was her only friend and to have fun with it. I say great. She also says that she really liked my scene with Mara and that she had learned something about her character from watching it in the dailies.

By the way, I never go to dailies because for me... I feel it can be dangerous to some actors. It makes me too aware of the way I look and distracts me from the intentions of the scene. But some actors, such as Faye, go every day.

Richard comes and visits for about half an hour. Barbara, Frank P.'s wife, had just arrived from N.Y., so I introduce her to Richard and she remembers him from Montana, where he had worked with Frank P. in a movie, *Rancho Deluxe* (1975). Later, Frank P. and I talk and I mention it. He says she should remember him, since he made an "indelible impression." (It was during a turbulent time in Richard's life and he was drinking heavily.) We talk about how Richard feels that their lives had paralleled somewhat. Frank agrees. Frank raves again about how talented Richard is. Frank Y. gives me a kiss again and mentions my sweet smile. David Koontz is there, too. We talk about his white grape vineyard ranch up north, his witnessing the birth of a baby lamb, and Christina killing her first chicken by holding its head on a wooden block and chopping it off with a sharp axe. ("Carol Ann, bring me the axe!")

I wrap at 12:30 a.m. Get the driver to take me home. I arrive at 1 a.m. to find an ogre: Richard scares me so much, he is furious that I didn't wait at the set for him. He had made a trip down and back and beat me home. He carries on and on and then goes to bed. I was scared to kiss him goodnight and mad as hell, too. I think he was totally unfair and overreacting.

I knit for a while and go to sleep at 2:30. A restless, sleepless night. Makes me wish that I had followed my earlier instincts about not having him in L.A. I feel that he is jealous that I am working and he's not. He's not supportive at all. It's all about him.

Saturday, February 14th

Valentine's Day. I awake at 9:30 a.m. Tired. I walk into the living room and Richard says sweetly did you kiss me goodnight last night? No, I say, and walk right past him into the kitchen. He comes and kisses me and hugs me. We make up. I open my gift, which last night he said if he'd had it in the car with him, he'd have thrown it out the window. It is Arpège perfume. (Funny, because it doesn't smell good on me, but it was his mother's favorite.)

Beautiful. I make him a card by cutting up some Marmont stationery, then I hit the chair and choked a towel in front of him, calling them Richard to get the rest of my anger out. He laughs.

I go to Darn Yarn to finish up Frank's scarf—I need more yarn. Richard doesn't come with me to pick out his yarn for his scarf. He stays home and reads. Shop at Quinn's for a Valentine's steak and salad dinner for two. Call Joan R. later to talk.

Oh, last night, Michael, our A.D., had pointed out Mr. David Begelman, the crook who is now President of M.G.M., talking to Frank P. I said who says crime doesn't pay? Big crime, that is—it's the little schmuck who gets twenty years.

Sunday, February 15th

Out fishing with Harrison Starr. Catch a halibut, too small, throw it back, and then some tomcod—throw them back. We were supposed to go to Sam Peckinpah's for roasted rabbit, but Sam changed his mind, so we went home.

Monday, February 16th

President's Day. Do laundry. Take Kukums for walk around pool. Go out to our friends Bud and Karen's Agoura ranch for dinner. So beautiful and peaceful out here. Smell of horses, hay, and fresh air.

Tuesday, February 17th

Get up at 6 a.m. Richard drives me to location. Makeup call at 7:30. We get two veggie burritos before Richard leaves. I finish up makeup and hair around 9:30 a.m. Go to my trailer, review my scene, and then lay down till 11:30. Lunch call, sushi and watermelon. Afterward go to hair and makeup for a touch-up and get dressed in my wardrobe.

They take me by car to the shooting location. The white convertible Lincoln Continental is there, hitched to the back of the camera truck. I wasn't supposed to drive or control it—just get behind the wheel for the close-ups. They've lucked out because I know how to drive a stick shift—the owner of the car had been really concerned about it, lest I grind the gears and possibly ruin his beauty. I say don't worry, I learned to drive on an old '49

Chevy stick, so I'm asked to actually drive the car on the long shots.

Terry brings in the new *T.V. Guide* with Faye on the cover for the Evita Peron T.V. special and is showing it to everyone around, including Frank P. I ask Terry about Faye's little boy—I say I didn't know she had a baby. He says we don't talk about him, it's private. Vivienne later says he was adopted.

Frank P. talks to me before we shoot. He says to remember this scene is eight years later—the fan thing is gone and Carol Ann is tired. It's 5 a.m. I've been abused and haven't had a vacation in five years. Faye and I run lines. We shoot the rehearsal. She jogs next to the car. We do two more master takes, then Faye's close-up.

Afterward, she drives back with me in the car. She says they had a chance to rent a house here, but decided not to because it's too close to the road. She says she likes living in the flats close to Rodeo Drive for shopping. I say I like living at the Marmont—it's convenient, too. She asks if I was from New York. I say yes, West Eighty-Fifth Street. She says oh, then we can be friends—she used to live on West Ninetieth and Central Park West, but they bought a home on Ninety-Fourth near Madison Avenue, just across from the Park. She says she loves New York and London. I tell her Elia Kazan said to give her his love. She asks when did I work for him, I tell her and I mention that I was Barbara Loden's friend, that's how I got to know him as a friend, but I did work with him in *The Last Tycoon*. Faye says she couldn't ever direct, but Streisand is directing in *Yentel* and she's probably going to do a good job. I tell her I didn't think directing was for me either, but that Barbara Loden was a wonderful director. She says you must tell me about it sometime. I don't say anything else. Before she goes, Faye also tells me I should have my scarf pressed before my close-up.

I ask Teresa to press it, but she would have to go back to base camp and there isn't time. So, I tell Frank P. that if the audience were to look at my scarf, I would be in trouble. He says we would all be in trouble if they're focusing on that and that he likes it just the way it is.

We do the close-up and then a master in reverse, then we took the location to the house exterior. I get on the people mover—we get lost for a few minutes going up the little winding roads. Then I do the shot driving up the driveway. First shot, I hit the curb and the car chugs all the way back up the hill. Faye thinks it was funny. We do one more take, which went well.

Before we lose the light to do the last take of us going away from the house, Frank P. comes up to me and says I was sensational, also a sensational person. Frank Y. teases me about going downhill, "The brake is the second pedal on the right."

I point to the gas—"You mean this one?"

"Yes, we'll write in Carol Ann's death scene tomorrow."

I hike up my skirt to my knee as I get in—a few whistles for Carol Ann and we do the scene. Wrap.

I get a ride home. Richard looks very sad. We go to the Olympic boxing stadium for the fights with Paul J. and Sally. "Little Red" Lopez is there. After we leave, we run into my friend, Warren, who's singing a little song while playing a car antenna bass. He's a little looped and sad and funny. Drop Paul off. Go home.

I have a huge headache. Richard watches T.V.

Wednesday, February 18th

En route to Gerald Schneider for a facial massage. He's excellent. In the building, I brush my black bag against the wall, getting wet paint all over it. There were no signs. I am mad. I wait for the guy to come with the paint remover but he is so slow I am afraid I'll miss my appointment. When he comes back, I leave the purse with him. He says if it doesn't work, they'd buy me a new purse. It comes out okay—smells like hell, but that'll wear off. Richard mails his picture off to *The Players' Guide*, special delivery. We meet Sonja and David Garfield at Imperial Gardens. Nice restaurant. We have a good time, they come up to our apartment afterward.

Thursday, February 19th

A lot of errands today, including the Department of Motor Vehicles. I go to the office for check, but it's not ready. Talk to Mauri and have lunch at Oblatt's. Briefly saw Nicholas Colasanto again. (In the '70s, Nic told me the story of his brief marriage: He had a heart attack right after the wedding and was rushed to the hospital, where his new wife started complaining about now not being able to go someplace in the Caribbean for their honeymoon. That night, he asked for a divorce.)

Go to bank for money to wire to New York, have to pay bills. See Sam Peckinpah after dinner. Drive out to his place, a trailer in Paradise Cove, around 9 p.m. Can't find a grocery store open anywhere for ice cream. Richard brings his cooked artichoke. We get there about 10 p.m. Sam is glad to see us. Gives me some good Tennessee whiskey. Listen to some female vocalist. She's good. He has the cassette and a Sony headset. Sam listens to two of Richard's Peter Tosh cassettes—two songs only, before going to the bathroom to cut up two white pills.

"Should you be taking these?" I say. I don't know what they are, but I suspect no good.

Sam asks Richard to bring him a glass of Clorox. He does—he put in a little bit of the pill that he had chopped up with his driver's license. It drifts down. Sam offers us some. I say no, I have to work, and Richard almost does, but hesitates. I kick his foot and say to Sam no, Richard's just come off a lot of drugs and is clean. Richard says no for himself. I am so proud of him. It turns out to be coke—Sam makes a reference about how this coke's not half-bad (attempting to dissolve a bit in bleach is, apparently, a popular do-it-yourself purity test). He talks until 12:15 a.m. I don't understand most of what he says. He's on another planet.

He shows us a poem he wrote and a Christmas card he received. He also has our Christmas card there that we had sent him last year. His Bible is open and I mention it, he says he reads it all the time, which surprises me. It's open to Ezekiel, and a lot of other parts have paper markers in them. He shows Richard a film magazine article on himself and says Richard's name is also in it.

It's sad to see Sam. He speaks of his terrible experience in the hospital, when he had his heart attack; he says that they tortured him and a sadistic pregnant nurse brought him back twice from the dead. I ask him how he feels about Steve McQueen's death—he says he cheated him, they were supposed to do another film together. Sam had wanted him for *Convoy* (1978) and he had wanted him for *Tom Horn* (1980). It's sad to see Sam go back to a life of drugs. He says he likes seeing us together, he likes couples who have made it, 'cause he never has. He says he's only known three.

That's about all I can remember of the conversation, most of it was incoherent. We drive home and get in a little after 1 a.m. I have to get up at 8 a.m. for work. Got a big day ahead.

Friday, February 20th

Work call 10 a.m. Go to makeup and hair. Vivienne's not feeling well but hair turns out the best yet.

Today we shoot the finding-Joan-drunk-scene. Diana is there. I'm a little envious of her being nominated for an Oscar after her first role. I wish it had happened to me, but I decide to put that all behind and be happy for her and go on with my scene with Faye and Diana.

We go to the set for rehearsal and Frank P. is there. I wrapped the muffler I knitted for him with pretty clown paper and a big colorful bow and give it to him after camera rehearsal. He tells me to wait a minute until he can open it privately. He comes back after five minutes and we sit on the couch and he opens it. Frank just loves it. It's a mauve colored yarn with great texture and little bits of other colors. He says it looks like a Missoni scarf, puts it on, and wears it around the set. He gets so many nice compliments. Someone says it looks like Hawaiian leis. Paul, the D.P., says oh, you finally came out of the closet. Frank tells everyone that I made it and that it was the first thing I've ever knitted.

After lunch from 3 to 4 we do our first shot. Diana has trouble slowing down for the camera on the entrance we make when finding Joan drunk. Faye is something else. Even "out of it," she won't just lie there. She plays to the camera and gets in additional dialogue she's made up when we help her stand. Diana is a good crier. She weeps well. She keeps it weepy, so I decide to change the delivery of my lines to her, to make them sharper and put in some conflict with her. I feel good about that. Then Diana loses the conflict by acquiescing too soon, so I tell her to keep it up. Faye wants to have a moment when we pick her up, so I said, "Let me know how I can help you." Faye calls me her fragile one. Frank says my strength comes through in the scene. I start losing my energy around 7:30 p.m. It is a struggle to keep it going. We wrap at 9:55 p.m. I feel it went well. Frank thanks me for the contribution I was making to the film and says he thinks it will be really good. I think so, too. Frank Y. thanks me. One of the crew comes up and tells me I'd done a good job. I feel I had held my own with the two other actresses, the rest is up to the editor.

There is Chinese food on the set. I call Richard to come and pick me up and have a Japanese beer and Chinese food and talk to some people. Richard comes at 10:30. We say goodnight to Frank and Frank and go to Roger Vadim's (film maker and former husband of Jane Fonda) art show at a gallery on Melrose Avenue, but Paul J., who invited us, has already left. Warren Miller is there, drunk. Susan Strasberg is there hunting for a man, as are a lot of other women. Vadim's paintings all feel shallow.

Richard wants to leave by the back way. I make him come back and we leave through the front door. Two fans get Richard for autographs outside. At first he doesn't want to, but they know his name and two of his movies, so he signs. Another guy wants one too. Richard says, "Do you even know who I am?" He doesn't, so Richards says no. He persists and Richard tells him to fuck off.

We leave and go home and then for a walk up the Strip. Lots of hookers are out. We go up to Carlos and Charlie's and the disco, but it's a private event. Walk back and go to sleep.

Saturday, February 21st

Wake up before Richard at 9:30 and do bills and letters. We relax and go out in the afternoon. Meet Paul J. at Schwab's and I walk back for a short nap. Dinner at Gene Elman's at 7:30. Nice evening, but draining.

Sunday, February 22nd

Took a Japanese cooking class that I had signed up for.

Monday, February 23rd

8:45 a.m. arrival for 9 a.m. call. Hilda gives me a manicure and then I head to hair and makeup. We rehearse at 12:45. Break at 1 for lunch, then shoot scene. It's the scene where we cut out Steve Forrest's head from all the photographs. Faye starts improvising some of it—she is irritated that the prop people cut out the heads for us and we have very few pictures left to work with. She says don't do that again. She has me give her photos in two places, one after she takes aspirin and the other after the children leave. Then I show her with a picture with Steve's face gone and she says, "For heaven's sake, Carol Ann, just cut the picture in half."

"I can't do that," I say, "the corners are already in the album," and she laughs. This was just a line that slipped out as we were shooting and Faye loves it, so I keep it. We try it different ways and at one point little Christopher trips on his way out—I felt the scene went well. I thank Faye afterward and she thanks me. She tells me that she would have to teach me about the camera the way Anthony Quinn had taught her. (She never did.) She tells Richard on the way out "She's really good," and Richard says "Yes, I know." Frank P. thanks me again for the scarf and says he'll wear it for the rest of his life. That touches me deeply.

Oh, while I was looking at photos of Faye as Joan, which her boyfriend, Terry O'Neill, had brilliantly shot, Terry came over and I asked him if I could have a photo of Faye as Joan, it would mean a lot to me. He said he would shoot us together. (Unfortunately, that never happened either.)

Richard and I go up to David Koontz's office and talk. David asks, strictly privately, if I think the little Christina was coming off as a brat. He is concerned about her performance, that maybe she isn't sweet enough. Richard says he doesn't like Mara—she is like a little snot. I say it didn't come off that way working with her, that I like her. David says he is concerned in one scene with the dolls that she came off hard, but he also says that the editor, Richard Harris, said not to worry, he can cut around it. (I knew deep down what they were getting at: There is a hardness in the performance that seems wrong for little Christina. She is too knowing, too wise, too much a professional little actress, there was not a simple sweetness there, but what was there to do, redirect and reshoot it?)

David also says not to worry that my scenes have been running long, because the editor also said it'll cut just right. I say that's better than if they're so quick you can't cut—have to have the moments, not going to worry about anyone's time clock.

Before we leave, he invites us to his country ranch to work for a weekend. He says we'd be roughing it. We say okay.

Go home, watch part one of *Evita* with Faye. Very well done.

Tuesday, February 24th

Vivienne tells me she thinks I look real pretty. First time she's seen me with lipstick. Frank P. had told me early on that I can't look pretty or attractive or Faye would have me fired. As I leave, Frank Y. comes in. We kiss on the cheeks and his secretary, actually named Carol Ann, gives him a message that gossip columnist Rona Barrett called. Everyone is trying to get the scoop on the film.

I meet Richard at Oblatt's for tacos. Do errands the rest of the afternoon, as I am off. Buy cute cat and dog picture books for Popi (my father) and his wife, Velta, which are not available in the Soviet Union. Watch part two of *Evita*, also very good.

Wednesday, February 25th

Appointment with Gerald Schneider for my skin. Rainy day. Richard cooks eggs and bacon breakfast when I get back before leaving to go to a boat show with Harrison Starr. I call Paramount and Alice, the bookkeeper, to check on my deductions. Got $116 more a week back. Good. Go to Crystal Palace and try on some clothes, buy some rhinestone earrings. Go to other antique stores but don't buy anything except a "Snatch a Watch" for Richard—you open it and a girl with fuzz on her pussy pops out.

Back home, Kukums crawls on my lap and Warren Miller calls about an agent taking his book to sell. Richard comes in and we leave to pick up Froma Sand, my former therapist. Take her to Nucleus Nuance, a small hip organic restaurant and jazz club tucked away privately. We have steak, she has veal. They've redecorated in the '20s Art Deco style. Nice. Froma gets dizzy if a room is too hot and several times feels bad, but she improves. She looks very good. Talks about "divorcing Hollywood" and the heartbreaks of coming so close, so close. (She was a screen writer and had several projects optioned—she also submitted her pilot script "Harry the Housekeeper" and found out later that it had been copied and was now called *Who's the Boss?* and had someone else's name on it. Froma sued and apparently got a $100,000 settlement, a pittance considering how long the show ran. Theft in Hollywood pays.)

Drop off Froma. Stop by and spend some time with Warren.

He shows us his newel post from Edwin Booth's estate. Head home.

Thursday, February 26th

Sam Shepard comes by for a visit. Richard had run into him in lobby. He was on his way up north to his house, but stopped in to check on rates at the Marmont. He talks about Joe Papp (a big theatrical producer in New York who produced a lot of Sam's plays) and being through with him. The last play they did was a disaster and he's going to recast it in San Francisco, doing it there and then bringing it to Marshall Mason's Circle Repertory Theater later this year. So hush-hush that Papp doesn't know about it yet. Doesn't want us to tell anyone.

He talks about really being conscious of aging, and not wanting to. He says he notices it with his parents. He is also in a quandary about change: He's struggling to leave his marriage of many years, but it's the years of commitment that he's invested. I think this might be about his romance with Jessica Lange coming to a head. Sam asks Richard's advice as to what he should do and what direction he should go—yes, should he leave his wife and marriage for Jessica Lange? He's quite distressed, very upset and near sobbing. Richard tries to make Sam feel better by telling him what a good writer he is and that Richard wished he could write. Sam says, "Oh, it's easy, just take a lot of amphetamines and you can finish a script in three days." (I worked with Sam in 1994 on *Safe Passage*, and he didn't remember me, just thought I looked familiar. That's show business for you.)

Call Patti at Michael Cimino's office, leave message about getting lunch. Mail books to Popi and Velta.

Friday, February 27th

Work call 10 a.m. Do makeup and hair. I sleep in my dressing room for about an hour, very carefully so my hair's not mussed. I brought Vivienne that organic hair spray and it had worked fine. Break for lunch at 1:30. Find out that we won't be doing the '40s shot; back to 1939 and when Christina the baby is first brought home, so have to re-do hair, which is down when rehearsal is called. Frank P. just loves my hair down, thinks it looks so pretty. I ask if I could wear it down. He says, "I'm afraid it would be too competitive with Faye."

When I give Frank a hug, Jonathan whispers something—I think he said not to get too close to Frank, 'cause he had the flu. I say it's okay, I'm immune, I already had the flu. They both say that's not what they're talking about. I go up to Jonathan and ask what were you talking about? He says Faye.

Later, we rehearse with a doll and save the real baby for the shot. They can only use a live baby for so many minutes a day. It goes well. The hair people (ours, not Faye's) all complain about Faye's wig behind her back, that she looks like a floozy. The makeup man complains that she looked too white—the makeup is too white. I ask who does this for her, they say she and her people. Otherwise, I stay out of it.

The crew has to light the new set, Crawford's living room, staircase, doorway, dining room. It's a magnificent set. Real art pieces. Frank Y. has even rented a real diamond pin for Faye to wear in this scene on her wrist. It takes nearly two hours for them to light it.

Faye's secretary asks me to come by at Faye's request to teach her to purl. I knock on the door and enter. She's painting her nails. I sit and take the little blue sweater she's started and start to show her how it's done.

Terry comes in and we talk about Barbara Loden's death, how long had she been ill, and Elia. Faye says she's sorry she never got to know Barbara better. Faye asks me if I work a lot, I tell her there are some dry spells in between. I tell her the last play I did and about the plays I worked on with Barbara. I tell Faye I think she was magnificent in *Evita* and how entertaining Richard and I thought it was, and how we felt it should be released as a film. She is unhappy with how it was edited—she feels the best scenes were left out, notes that the director also didn't like it, and that they want to re-edit it themselves and release it.

Faye again mentions that I'm from New York to Terry, and I say we'd like to have them over in New York. They both say fine. I don't remember how the subject came up with antiques. Oh, I think it was because they often antique hunt on Columbus Avenue. I mention the apricot lamp we just bought in New York.

Faye says apricot is her favorite color. Noted.

I mention the Pickfair auction (Pickfair was the famous, lavish home of Mary Pickford and Douglas Fairbanks, when they were married.) There is an auction of the contents of the home on Saturday, and they say they'd like to go. I tell Terry I'll get the info from Richard for them.

Faye picks up the purl stitch very quickly but tends to invert it—I don't know if that makes much difference. But she's quick. I tell her just to practice it over the weekend, it took me a few days to get it. She mentions perhaps wanting a lesson with my teacher, so I tell her of Darn Yarn.

Faye mentions to Terry her wish that they could go home now. What's taking so long? They must talk to the production people about this. Then Faye says she wants to get ready—a signal for me to leave. Was in there for over thirty minutes. I notice that I'd been a little nervous and had sweat a little.

We go on to shoot the scene and then I stay for off-camera for Faye. The stage was freezing. Frank Y. sees me and says I could go now. 8 p.m. They had just ordered pizza and I call Richard to tell him to come by at 9. My per diem check had been sent over by Tim and I'm all set to go with Vivienne to take my hair down when the A.D. rushes over and says I'm not done and they might need me. About 9 p.m., they are doing an over-the-shoulder on Faye and Frank P. has me work in the background, but I'm not seen on camera. Frank P. apologizes to me. I say, "Look, I'm getting overtime and pizza, I'm happy." It then occurs to me that everyone, including the crew, is getting meal penalties and overtime—no wonder Frank Y. looks a little worried.

I go to my trailer to have my robe fitted and then back to hair, take the pins out, and back on stage. Sign out 9:25 p.m. and wait for Richard. Frank and Frank talk. Victoria's (Faye's stand in) little girl is on set and at the moment is sitting in my chair. I let her.

Waiting. Getting worried. It's 9:45. I tell Mauri I'm worried Richard may have had a car accident. She calls the gate to make sure he didn't have trouble getting in, then looks out and sees Richard standing there and calls him in. He looks a little off. I immediately sense that he took cocaine and quietly confront him. He denies it. Then admits it. I ask him who he got it from. He tells me that girl I don't like and I ask him how much he spent. He says twenty. I don't believe him. I'm furious at him, but contain myself till we're in the car. I drive home. Later I find out he lied to me about the money, it cost a lot, lot, lot more. Lying hurts. We go to sleep.

At least Richard had given Terry O'Neill the letter about the Pickfair auction and had seen Frank P. on his way out.

Oh, earlier, the temporary school teacher had told me I looked like Lily Tomlin's Ernestine character with my hair net—I told her I had no intention of looking like that and for her not to tell me that, it doesn't make me happy. Later, I told Vivienne and she got furious that she had said that. I said she's ignorant. Vivienne said it was lucky she didn't say it to Diana Scarwid, she probably would have burst into tears, she's so sensitive.

"Let's tell that teacher her braids look awful," Kathy said.

I said to just forget it.

Saturday, February 28th

Rainy day. Some errands. Go shopping and look at the men's stores. Visit Warren Miller, we have coffee; he puts it over the heater to keep the pot warm. Go to a Japanese double-bill film afterward. The Japanese man who runs the theater talks to Richard about a karate script he has. Richard gave him Chuck Norris' info. Head home, watch T.V., and go to sleep.

Sunday, March 1st

Raining hard this morning. No fishing. Stay in all day. Reread the script and my scenes.

Monday, March 2nd

See films *Melvin and Howard* and *Private Benjamin* and admit that Goldie's hair does look great, but it's definitely not Joan Crawford's. Run into Froma's friend, Stewart.

Tuesday, March 3rd

Richard and I go to Gerald Schneider's for my skin care and for chiropractic adjustment, then over to the agency to pick up a check, then to Fox to visit Paul Jenkins on the set of *Dynasty*, where he had a small, sometimes-recurring role. Linda Evans is giving Richard the eye, she really likes him. Light dinner at Mirabelle and Paul tells us the story of his weekend—a real disaster. He says he'd gone up to Big Sur with Diane Silver, a producer. He says she was "A neurotic, castrating bitch." I ask him why he allowed himself to be treated so badly, he says he wanted to use her to get work. Oh, Hollywood.

Wednesday, March 4th

7 a.m. work call to parking lot of Methodist Church on Wilshire Boulevard by Beverly Glen. There are about eight extra ladies for the fan club scene and they think I'm one, too. When we get to the breakfast wagon, the food guy is very rude about my ordering a veggie burrito. He says he couldn't do it. I persist and he finally does with a bad attitude. It's the extras who get treated badly. If an extra lady wanted one, why not? She should be able to.

We get makeup and are taken up by the people-mover to a Bel Air house of some doctor. I bet he's a plastic surgeon. There's a swimming pool building here that I could live in, the pool itself, and a tremendous yard about a half-block long, and a house on top of the hill. The house is off-limits to everyone but Faye and we could go to the pool house only. It is freezing cold and rainy, but then the rain holds off. We shoot the fan mail sequence. I have a little improvisation moment with Mara about not putting so much water on the stamps. They pull little Jeremy—it is all women now. Faye comes out. She singles out one of the extras to talk to in the scene before she comes to Mara and me. The extra girl is just thrilled and asks for a Polaroid with her.

I get through at noon and one of the extra ladies, Joyce, needs a ride to Highland and Sunset, so I take her. She offers to give me gas money. I refuse. The extras work so hard for their money. After my scene she congratulated me—I said for what? She said for our little scene, that every bit helps. She is a tubby girl with terrible pimples on her face. I feel like telling her to go to a good dermatologist, but I don't. She turns out to be a singer and dancer who also teaches dance and did the mother in the musical "George M!" in Las Vegas.

Get home. Richard and I go out to get Chinese food and bring it back to eat here. They put MSG or something in it—I get numb cheeks and jaw, Richard has a bad headache.

Thursday, March 5th

7 a.m. call. Heavy rain today. Yesterday, I nearly had an accident skidding through a stop sign. Brakes would not hold. They made arrangements for a new car to be delivered and exchanged at 1 p.m. I changed it to 3, because Richard was out on two interviews. The studio was supposed to pick me up at 6:45. No driver.

A man comes to the door in shorts and sweat shirt. I say, are you my driver? He is taken aback. He is a guest. I say I guess not, sorry. Get on the phone and call the studio again. The man waits for me to get through and then apologizes for not being my driver. I say I'm sorry I mistook you. He says would a driver look like this? I say yes—young and energetic.

The driver arrives at 7:15. Get to the studio at 7:30. Frank Y. asks me if I am enjoying my stay. I say yes, I have a great view of a billboard from my window. They just changed it from *Stir Crazy* to *American Pop*. Eileen asks if we would have a billboard for *Mommie Dearest*. Frank says yes. Eileen asks if it is good for business. Frank says it is good for his ego. I say how exciting it was to see the big billboard at Times Square for *The Deer Hunter*. Frank said he put the big one up there for *The Godfather* when he was President of Paramount (1971-1975).

We do the eating scenes today—the rare prime rib, the one that little Christina refuses to eat—it is delicious. Later in the afternoon, we shoot the breakfast scene. They cooked eggs for us, and bacon, sausage, strawberries, French bread, toasted—fabulous. I'm stuffed! I take Richard for a tour of the living room set and we see Frank Y. talking to Terry. Richard goes over and says hello and thanks Frank for treating me so nicely. I tell Frank that he is the last of the class act guys. Frank tells me I should get a lot of work from this film. I say I hope so. Harry Goz is on the set. We talk about agents—he left I.C.M. after eleven years and is doing better than ever. He also saw a play I did in New York. He had a friend, Jimmy Dukes, in the show. I tell him I had seen him do the lead in "Fiddler on the Roof" years ago on Broadway. He was wonderful.

David Koontz comes over. I tell him he just missed seeing Richard looking so handsome. He had bought a new $25 tie—beautiful. Vivienne says she did a double-take. David says I look very good in the film. I say I thought the eating scene with Mara went very well. He thanks me for saying that. Harry Goz starts asking David about Al Steele, the character he is playing, why he did certain things. David says that so much of that is directorial and he doesn't feel he should get into that.

I leave to go rehearse. Steve Forrest comes in and says I look good. My hair is parted in the center with the two side rolls. A crew guy had told me I looked like a picture of his mother.

I finish at 7:05 p.m. and have the driver to take me home. Richard goes over his scene with me a number of times. Paul J. comes over for a brief visit. Fix soup and franks and cabbage. Go to bed at midnight.

Oh, my last scene was the pick-up shot: "I'm sorry Joan, can, can you go back to sleep?" Of course, Faye was not there. Did this in two takes. (And if you don't remember it, it's because it was cut.)

Friday, March 6th

Up at 6 a.m. Richard takes me to work then goes home to get ready for his audition. I feel for him 'cause I know he's nervous. I search for the right words to say to comfort him. They elude me. I reach into my pocket and find the penny I found yesterday and make a wish for Richard.

Am tired today. Hope it doesn't affect my work too badly. Am greeted by an actress, Alice Nunn—the loud and aggressive one. I avoid her. Conversation minimal. When she leaves, Vivienne says, "Bossy, isn't she?"

I agree.

"I wouldn't want to be around her too long."

I agree and then add that I'm sure she'll be very good in her part. She has a great character face. I go to the set. Alice corners Faye. Faye introduces herself to Alice very graciously but then Alice is like a bulldozer. I feel Faye back off.

We do the scene where we come in from jogging and Faye gets a call from Steve Forrest. After the first take, Frank says to me be less excited about "sexy Mr. Savitt." More subtle. Okay. The scene goes much faster than they expected. When Faye gets the part and she gets excited, she whirls me around and runs up the stairs. The best take was the one the cameraman blew, but I think they can use half of it. I had a problem keeping the baby Christopher from crying. Faye says we could do an insert of me at the stairs where she throws the towel and also in one take put the towel around my neck. That's generous of her and Frank P. picks up on it right away.

Oh, yesterday when Frank P. did the reading as Joan (because Faye didn't stay for my close-up), and after my take Frank Y. said, "God, you're good, Rutanya, to act with that terrible line reading." I said it was a good reading, he's good. Faye is never there.

We break for lunch at 12:50. Talk to Richard during lunch. Richard sounds low, his reading didn't go as well as he wanted it to. I feel so bad for him. Whenever he feels this way a drug binge is coming up. Oh God! Sometimes I just don't know if I am going to get through this.

I eat and go to lie down in my dressing room. I sleep from 1:30 to 3:30. So tired and in the middle of my period. Teresa wakes me up, then Amy by accident delivers my wardrobe for the floor scrubbing scene, which we won't be doing today.

They wrap me at 4:45. Get a driver to take me home at 5 p.m. Richard left a message that he's with Paul J. I know what that means. Paul J. supplies Richard with the drugs. My stomach takes a dip. Kendall calls. Jeff Hunter, my N.Y. agent, called yesterday, but he's too busy to get together even though he is here in L.A. I'm double ticked off.

Earlier, Frank Y. had said to Frank P. that he was furious with David Koontz because of what was in Army Archerd's column. He said David leaked it, and Frank Y. wanted to control everything that went out about the film. It mentioned Diana Scarwid's move back home and all her movie offers and David being on the set every day and Christina visiting once to meet Diana and Mara (though Christina told me recently that she never, ever went to the set). I don't know quite why Frank was upset.

Steve Forrest also came in to do the telephone voice dressed up like a cowboy—he was going riding afterward. He hinted again that he'd had a rough night last night fooling around. He had been interested in Robin and I introduced them. I asked him how he gets away with it all. He said he has an understanding wife who is a great success at real estate. She just sold a million-and-a-half dollar house and bought him a Mercedes. They're married thirty-two years and have three grown sons. Steve also said he had a great dirty joke but couldn't tell me. He talked about his father being a Baptist minister, wouldn't let them go to dances or movies.

Then, Terry O'Neill brought in 11-by-14-inches black and white photos of Faye as Joan in her 50s or 60s. It was a startlingly close expression and look that he caught. I congratulated him and he said, "Oh, it's her. She does it all. I just shoot it." Frank P. and Frank Y. both liked it. Frank Y. said he wouldn't mind having it be the cover of *Time* magazine.

I spoke to Faye while we were waiting to go on camera. She said to me, "You don't go to rushes do you?" I said no, and she asked why not? I said I just didn't like the way I look watching myself. She said she was like that way on *Bonnie and Clyde* for about two weeks and "You just get critical." I said she sure does know the camera and lighting and how much I respected that. She said you have to protect yourself—they don't light the way they used to in Joan's time.

Saturday, March 7th

Go to Beverly Hills and buy a beautiful hand-made sweater for myself. I might as well spend some money on myself, because I can see it just going to Richard's drugs if I don't.

Sunday, March 8th

Get up and get on the road by 11 a.m. to go to the Santa Anita Races. The Santa Anita Handicap was on. Hot day, about 100,000 people there, like New York on New Year's Eve. Richard gets upset with the crowds, running back and forth with no place to sit. About the fourth race we ran into Karen and Boyd Z., our friends from the Agoura ranch, who were there by the rail. Richard brightens up. (Boyd had been his close friend since eighteen.) We win forty-eight dollars on a two-dollar bet on the fifth race. The father of the horse was named "Pie King."

Get home at 6:30. Call Froma to say we'd be late, go to Numero Uno to get two pizzas, then have a nice time with her friends. Her daughter calls from Texas to say she's getting married. The phone's passed around. Richard missed the married part and wishes her a happy birthday and then thinks she's getting a divorce.

Froma tells stories, including the Victor Mature story: When meeting Victor to interview him early in her career as a writer, he took out his enormous cock and showed it to Froma.

"Would you like to do something with this?"

"Congratulations, that's the biggest penis I have seen in my life, but I never mix business with pleasure."

Monday, March 9th

Mauri calls to say they will not need me today, so we drive out to Woodland Hills for lunch with the Duvall family. (Dr. Albert Duvall had been a world renowned Reichian therapist and my therapist for many years. He had recently passed away.) It feels good to spend time with them. It is sad but good to see Jeanette and Cheryl again, Albert's wife and daughter. Jeanette shows me Albert's photo that she had blown up and gives me a copy. She talks about Albert's last days, how he went back to touching materials and fabrics. Fabrics were his toys as a little boy and as a little child he loved to touch them. So, in his last days, he reverted to touching the fabrics of his family and the fabrics of everyone around him.

We head out to lunch at a restaurant. Jeannette says had Albert lived he would have combined orgonomy (Reichian therapy) with nutrition. Chanda, their granddaughter, is home when we return and she gives Richard and me a letter saying how much she likes us. Later she takes me into her room and shows me her Paddington Bear that Albert had given her before he died and books about Paddington's adventures. She gives me a little tiny monkey. We all take photos and leave.

Later, Richard Ross, our attorney, and his girl, Lela, meet us at the Marmont and we go to Matoi's for dinner. They come back for a half-hour to visit in our room. They absolutely adore Kukums.

Tuesday, March 10th

7 a.m. work call. Richard drops me off on Beverly Glen Boulevard for Christina's birthday party scene. The house is a

magnificent place on the Boulevard. We have breakfast and the food guy asks me twice how I liked my veggie burrito. I guess he's gotten the message that I was not an extra. Richard leaves.

I go to hair and makeup. First time that my hair is down. Vivienne is a little concerned about Faye being jealous of my hair down, but as I sit there Terry comes in and says he thought for a moment I was the star, I looked so pretty. I say no way. Faye notices it right away. She looks pretty in her pinafore—a matching outfit with Mara. Lots of pretty things on the set: carousel, ponies, clown, man with a monkey, the weirdest monkey. It sat so still all day long, only its eyes moved. Someone thought it may have been drugged. It only shook hands when a coin was put into the cup. Faye noticed how delicate the monkey's fingernails were—like a tiny old woman's. Then the monkey offered his foot to Faye and she drew back, scared.

I have the scene where I hand the baby to Faye. I improvise a little in each handing. The baby is teething and almost cried once but other than that he is a very good baby. Beautiful day. Four soldier extras are behind me. Faye checks out their rank and stripes, identifying each of them right on. One extra has a full wig on and Frank P. has to position him so the back is not seen on camera. He does it with sensitivity.

Frank seems a little low all day. He comes over to sit with Vivienne and me and Vivienne asks him if he's tired. He says yes. She later says that he'd been short with everyone today and that was his way of making up. Victoria (Faye's photo double) says I look fantastic in the dress I had on and I should keep it. Frank says it's okay with him, but that I should ask the D.A. first. I ask what that is. He says the district attorney.

Toward the late afternoon, Frank seems to warm up. He says bring in the baby and I say here I am—I'm the baby. He laughs. An extra lady tells Faye with her makeup she looks so much like Joan. I say that Faye created it, 'cause in real life she doesn't look like Joan—she creates it. It seems to please Faye.

I have lunch in my trailer and lie down for half an hour. The strong Los Angeles sun can get to you.

We wrap at 5:30 p.m. I have to wait a bit and then get a ride home with Mara's car. Richard and I go out to get Chinese and bring it back. Richard seems a little odd, so I question him and question him about what he'd done and whether it was coke. He denies all. I feel like I'm overdoing it. He says he is just tired and low. Kukums curls up in my lap. Richard is beside me on the couch. I think he's done drugs. I realize that I am happier on the set when I only have to deal with Carol Ann's life. My own life seems much more complicated by problems I don't want to face.

Wednesday, March 11th

Wake up 6 a.m. Went to sleep late yesterday. I can see why Faye is asleep by 9 and Frank Perry, too. Richard drops me off. I go to hair and makeup but it's not anyone I know. Weird. I ask a crew guy is the other makeup trailer in yet? He says guess not. It takes me a few minutes to discern the mansion is not the same one I shot in. I get very nervous. Turns out to be another film shooting two blocks away. I run and Vivienne and Charlie rib me for being fifteen minutes late.

The shoot is long. I just try to pace my energy. Don't talk too much. Have lunch in my trailer and try to nap but I can't. Vivienne combs me out. While she's putting the pins in, one of the hair ladies complains about the amount of drugs on movie and T.V. sets. I say I guess the *T.V. Guide* article on drug use on Hollywood sets is true. She says oh yes, and more. She just left *Under the Rainbow* (1981) because drugs were everywhere. Crewmembers had complained to the producer but he chose not to do anything. Also, the hairdresser who was doing one of the stars' hair is terrified, she says, because he put a pistol between her legs and rubbed it up and down. She says he's on drugs a lot and very unpredictable. Also, they hated David Carradine in particular and were terrified of his extreme mood changes when working because of drugs.

I come back to set and Faye and I pose for two pictures with my camera. Then we do some more long shots and a close-up with the baby. Terry comes and introduces me to the *L.A. Times* reporter, which is sweet of him, and then he takes him over to Faye. She's very charming with him.

When the shot is over, Terry takes photos of Faye with the four soldiers. I ask Terry for the photo of me and Faye that he had told me he would take. He says when we get back to the studio, he knows what he wants to do (but never did). Well, Faye is through but I have to stay for some hand-held camera shots of the people at various scenes during the party. I don't know if any of it will be seen, but I pick some specific things to do: Go supervise the carousel, check with the photographer to make sure he takes a picture of each child, give Mara a balloon, check the candles on the cake, tell Jimmy, the photographer, to take a shot of Mara on the carousel, all the things Carol Ann would do for Joan. (It all wound up on the cutting room floor.) Most of the people here don't do that at all, they're busy gossiping about themselves. One young grip is telling an extra girl that he wouldn't have shot the film that way, he doesn't like any of Frank Perry's shots. He'd just do it all hand-held. Stupid kid.

Get a ride back to the hotel. Richard's not at home. Sam Peckinpah calls and we plan on getting together. Richard gets in later. We have Chinese food and watch a little T.V.

Thursday, March 12th

Report to location at 7 a.m. on Beverly Glen for swimming scene. It was cloudy and cold. About 8:15 they decided to go to a cover set on Stage 16 back at Paramount, because we need two good, sunny days and tomorrow's supposed to rain. Richard brings me a bowl of oatmeal and kisses me goodbye.

I head back to Paramount and to Stage 16 with the driver and Amy and Teresa. We all fall asleep on the way. Get there early—no one is there yet. Paul, the D.P., brings obscenely good pastries with his arrival. I have a couple. I finally get a dressing room and heater.

They call rehearsal. The cleaning scene with Faye, Alice, and myself. Frank sits us on the couch. Alice spills coffee over the chair and rug. She's nervous. I tell her I couldn't tell. I don't want her to feel bad, it was an accident. Then Frank joins us, saying "I'm not going to get upset—I'm going to remain calm." We discuss the scene. I look for an object I could do and pick a glass and a rag to wipe it with. Faye smells good. I tell her. She says she just put on perfume.

We block with me in the scene, then Faye has me taken out of the scene to stand by the camera. Here she goes again, taking me out of scenes. At first I'm hurt and I know she picked up on it.

Then we break for ten and I decide I better change my hurt negative attitude, otherwise it will only hurt me. Plus Faye will pick up—she picks up quickly on negative vibes. I decide the positive thing happening is I'm learning about the camera. Faye knows the camera so well and I am learning from her. So, I go up to her and tell her. She says she should really take time with me, like Anthony Quinn took time with Faye to teach her. She's forgotten she had told me that before and it never happened, but I know Faye has picked up on my change. She has my eyes spotlighted as I stood beside the camera. "Those eyes, I have to see those eyes." The rest of the scene goes well. At one point, Alice and I get bunched up behind Faye as we're following her around. I think that was the best take. Frank tells us to step out on each side of her if that happens again.

I call Richard a couple of times. We only have a half-hour for lunch. Then we do the rest of the scenes. I miss a cue from Faye—it came so fast—I was supposed to run to my mark and deliver the line that Mr. Savitt was here. I barely made the mark. Frank tells me about missing it in front of everyone. I say I'm sorry. I get it next time. I wish he had told me quietly or privately, like Kazan did, and not yelled it out in front of the cast and crew.

It's 7:45 p.m. when Faye leaves. Time for my close-up. Faye tells Frank and Frank that she really needs twelve hours to rest because tomorrow will be a difficult day and she needs to look terrific. Frank Y. says he wants her to look good. Faye says she can give them 7:30 a.m. I go up to Faye as she was leaving. She says, "Love you." I ask her permission for my younger half-brother and his wife to visit tomorrow. (Everyone who visited the set had to have Faye's permission, as it was a closed set.) She says yes and yes to taking pictures with them.

I do my close-ups in two takes and get released. I ask Frank, aren't we going to do the shot with "Helga, let's go back to work"? Frank says, "Oh yes, we can't tonight, the crew would just get too upset, it's too late," but he told Marshall to get it at another time, to write it down.

I get a driver to take me back. While we were waiting for a shot, Michael, the A.D., and Frank Y. and I were sitting on a stairway. Michael was telling a story about Marty Ransohoff giving

Elizabeth Taylor a $20,000 diamond ring, because the film *The Sandpiper* (1965) she starred in did so well, and even before he was out the door Liz was saying bad things about him. Frank Y. says that he didn't pay for the ring himself. Still waiting. I take photos.

When I get home Richard has me sit on the chair. He was emotional. We talk about him having seen Jeanette Duvall (Dr. Duvall's widow was also a therapist) for a session. I fall asleep about 12:15 a.m., after a Häagen-Dazs feast.

Friday, March 13th

Lucky 13. Go to view items at the Pickfair auction. Fall in love with George Clausen's watercolor from 1885 in a beautiful frame. Hope to get it. Pick up my half-brother, Andy, and his wife, Eva, at the airport. Take them to Oblatt's for lunch and then to Paramount, Stage 31, where Faye is shooting the Louis B. Mayer scene. I go to get coffee with Eva and find a guard kicking Richard and Andy out. I stop it and tell him they've been cleared. He goes to check with Bob—just then, Faye, who is taking a break, spots us and comes over asking "Is this your family?" I introduce them and Andy says he's a great admirer of hers. She glows. I tell her they just about got kicked out. She laughs and says it's a difficult scene today. She has to break down and she isn't used to working on an open set. The office is open to the whole stage. I ask if we can take photos. She says yes and I run to get the camera in my bag, which I left on Charlie's makeup chair. We take three photos—I get anxious for the camera light to come on. Faye likes my sweater. I tell her Richard got it for me, which is a lie, and then give her secretary the name, address, and phone number of Darn Yarn.

I decide it's not a good idea to hang around for filming, as we may get kicked out if Faye gets tense, and out of respect for Faye, too. We leave and run into David Koontz, then walk down "New York Street" and take photos. We go to Quinn's for food shopping and then back to the Marmont, where I leave the chicken and potatoes in the oven as Richard and I race to get to the auction. We get there at 11 a.m. Get home, talk, go to sleep at 1:30 or 2 a.m.

Saturday, March 14th

Up at 8:30 a.m. to get to auction by 11. We're delayed and get there around 11:30, missing the porcelains. There are a lot of other things coming up including a lot of beautiful old trunks of Mary Pickford's. One of the stars of *Dallas*, Charlene Tilton, is bidding on everything, including the trunks. She pays $20,000 for a trunk on top of thousands for other things. We are stunned. Richard calls her Ms. Piggy.

Get back 6:30 p.m. and get ready for Pasquale's. We drive out to Malibu at 9:45 and catch the first jazz set. It lasts until 11:15 and then this comic friend of Richard's comes on, he's terrible but I admire his courage. I have two daiquiris and I'm sleepy. We go to the Atomic Cafe to eat and look at the punkers. Asleep at 2:30 a.m.

Sunday, March 15th

Up at 9:30 a.m., leave at 11:30 to get to auction by noon. I insist Richard gets gas. He gets pissed but does. (Richard had a lazy habit of running a car near empty and we had gotten stuck on roads and highways many times because of it.)

Richard asks the guard if we can invite Andy and Eva in, he says yes, so we bring them up. It's because Richard talked and made friends with the guards over the last two days.

Very high bidding today, the last day. The auctioneers are sharks. We buy a woodblock for $100, thinking we won't be able to afford the Clausen. The bidding on the Clausen starts at $500. My heart sinks as it goes to $600, $700, and then at the last minute I raise my hand for $800. I feel Richard jump. But then we get it. He's happy and I'm happy. Andy and Eva are happy for us. We don't have enough cash with us. We ask if we can pay for part of it now and come back tomorrow. She says no but she'll take a check, so I give her a check, and pass on the woodblock. A girl who works at the place comes up and thanks us for passing on it because now she gets it. I'm happy for her. She says she's an artist and those were her two favorites and she's happy the Clausen found a good home.

We go to pick it up and the girl lets it drop. My heart stops. Luckily it doesn't break, although I wonder if she chipped the frame a bit. We eat Chinese next door, then for a drive by Universal and up Mulholland. Come back and rest for an hour and go the movies to see *La Cage aux Folles II*.

Monday, March 16th

    Schwab's for breakfast. I forgot my visor and go back to pick it up, then gas up and go to Paradise Cove for fishing. We have to run to catch the boat. We thought it left at 1 p.m., but it leaves at 12:30 and we get there at 12:29. Andy and Eva both catch fish, then Richard catches one, then I get a big pull on the line. I don't think I can pull it up, so I ask Richard to do it. He does it very skillfully: A big fat halibut that's thirty inches long and over twenty pounds. We catch more halibut, but they are small, so we throw them back. It is a wonderful day on the water.

    We go back at 4:30 and the guy I'm sitting next to on the boat offers to buy our halibut for $15. I say I don't want to sell it, I want to eat it. We stop by Warren's to borrow a sharp knife and run into Paul J., who'll come by later. We have to go to Quinn's, too, because I forgot the oil and we show the fish to the girls working at the desk at the Marmont. Richard brings them two cooked pieces later, they sent back clean plates and a thank you note. Paul comes by to eat and we all have dinner. We're knocked out. Eva falls asleep. The rest watch T.V. till 12:30 a.m. I had called Bob Doherty twice and he finally confirmed I would not work tomorrow.

Tuesday, March 17th

    St. Patty's Day. Everyone got up at 10:30 a.m. We all needed the rest. Starving, we have lunch at Anna Marie's. Andy wanted Italian food. Bob calls to say they want me on set at 3 p.m. after all to do the pick-up shot they didn't get earlier, the one watching Faye and Steve go upstairs. (Without a cell phone, I always had to leave a phone number with production where I could be reached at any time, so I had looked up the restaurant's number in the Yellow Pages.) They drop me off at Paramount, then go do a few things before dropping Andy off at the airport. His flight leaves at 6:15 pm. We had gotten on his case last night and today about taking care of his teeth and having his cavities fixed. It was nice spending time with him. Eva is staying until Friday.

    Once we get to the set, we run into Diana Scarwid and I introduce them. I also tell everyone the story of catching the halibut and that I hadn't entered the jackpot on the boat. (They had an option to put in two bucks and the biggest catch won it all.)

Frank Y. says, "Oh, you always got to take a chance." He seems more upset than I am about my not entering. Frank P. says to me, "I bet you didn't think you would do this shot, either—I bet you didn't believe me when I said we would." I say oh, I believed him, I just didn't know when. He says he doesn't know if he believed it himself.

Ralph Nelson, the still photographer, and I compare being in airplane accidents. As a passenger, he was thrown through the window in a seaplane and cut his wrists, then swam three hundred yards in salt water to shore. He then learned to fly with money he got from the accident. I was on a plane that got wind-sheared and made a crash landing on the airfield. We slid down the yellow chutes and were told we were lucky to be alive. As I'm sitting and talking, they break for food, and Paul, the D.P., comes up to Tim Spencer, the camera operator, and says "If I don't get back in time, just do it for me" (which is just not done on a major motion picture).

"What should I shoot it at?"

"Oh, the same old shit," Paul says and walks away. Marshall, the script supervisor, says what a thing to say when the actress is sitting there. I realize they were talking about my shot and I resent deeply the attitude that is often under the surface here but just breached like a whale with Paul. Most of the people seem to be just clocking in—no artistry here, none wanted.

When I shoot my close-up, Faye and Steve are not there. I really miss them because they provide me with the living juice. So, I have to create my own with my imagination. I work on the subtext that would get my juices flowing and ask Victoria to stand in for Faye. We do three takes and the first was the best, but I didn't clean the glass as I did in rehearsal. I do on the third one, but I didn't feel it was as good as the first. Frank likes the kind of shudder I got in the first take. I feel my subtext was really working in the first take, and I didn't take the time in-between the others that I should have. I let myself get rushed because of the attitude of the crew. It was the last shot, and they wanted to go home and a couple vocalized it. Still, I did feel the first one was okay.

They wrap me. I have a driver bring me back to the Marmont and run into Bobby De Niro. He's late and in a hurry, but we talk.

He says he was in town for a while but didn't know if he'd be staying for the Academy Awards. He was here for a film he and Marty (Scorsese) were doing, *The King of Comedy* with Jerry Lewis. I ask if there was anything in it for us—he says he didn't think so, but he wanted to think about it and he'd let us know. I say fine.

Wednesday, March 18th

Richard's very low. I suspect it's the crash from being off drugs. Start of a full moon, too. Drop Eva off at Universal for the studio tour. Do errands. Pick her up. Eva and I drive to Palomino Club for the t-shirts and listen to the show and have a drink. It's nice just being there with her, without Richard. I'm having fun.

Zena, my elderly quilt-maker friend in Pasadena, calls late. She's now learning doll-making. What an amazing woman.

Thursday, March 19th

Rain. Get up 7:30 a.m. because I thought I heard the phone. Went back to sleep. Get up again at 11:30. Fix steak and eggs, shower, head to Janet Sartin for skin care. Eva gets her skin analyzed. We go to Paramount to pick up my check, then have Pizza. Head back. Paul J. stops in. Go to Harrison Starr's for dinner. First to arrive, last to leave. Home by 2 a.m. Go up Hollywood Boulevard to see low-riders, but none there, all quiet. Head home. Andy had called.

Yesterday, I read in the paper that Eleanor Perry, Frank's ex-wife, had died on the 14th of cancer in New York. That is why Frank looked so sad the week before and on Tuesday. I understand now why I had seen him be off by himself, with no good mornings to anyone. I remember watching his solitary shape and sensing something was very, very wrong.

Friday, March 20th

Eva packs as I take care of business calls. Richard calls Paramount and his agency, which creates huge anxiety in him. He seems to collapse and then becomes angry and snarling, which continues for hours. I've finally had it and get mad and leave to go to the bank, take Eva to the airport, and go to the Filmex festival. We drop by M.G.M. and pick up t-shirts for Eva and Andy.

Gertrude, the lady who works there, fell and hit her head. We help her. Soon I am saying bye to Eva.

Later, Richard cries as he tells me of his feelings. He asks me to understand and just go through the feeling with him—not try to fix it or solve it—but feel it with him. He says sometimes he feels I don't love him. He knows I do, but sometimes he feels it. He says that I'm too quick for him sometimes, he doesn't have my energy, that sometimes, if he didn't know better, he'd think I took amphetamines. We kiss and hug. I feel so bad for him, but he's right, sometimes I feel my love has been burnt by all the drug use, all the bank accounts that are emptied by it, all the hell that never seems to end. Oh, it ends for a while, but then starts up again like wildfire. I crawl into bed and sleep for three hours. I'm so depressed. I had been feeling good. I just can't take all the rage directed at me for so many hours, especially when I didn't feel it was deserved.

Saturday, March 21st

Get a call to work Monday 7 a.m. Richard went out to watch Paul J. fence. Granted, he is very good at this sport. I get up and am waiting for him when he gets in. I had taken Kukums out to eat some grass and the car to Aida Grey's salon for a facial treatment. Bella did it, turns out she recently emigrated from Riga. I tip her extra to help start her new life in America. I stop at Darn Yarn to get Faye's yarn for the scarf I want to make for her, but they don't have anything in apricot. However, there is a light rust with little white flowers in the yarn, lovely and delicate. I take it and start knitting by evening. It'll be beautiful. We spend the night in. I go get ice cream and we pig out.

Sunday, March 22nd

I wake up with a jolt. I hear something in Richard's voice. Something happened. I walk out of the bedroom, naked. We've been robbed, I'm told—not here, but in our New York apartment. Our new Sony T.V. is gone. But the odd thing is that our doors were locked. There are no open windows. It's either a lock picker or our landlord. We speak to Howard Rollins (the actor) and Denise (both neighbors). We're all upset. We decide that Richard will go back to New York to secure the apartment, put on new locks. I pack a black duffel bag with books and papers we'd be bringing back anyway. I give him the keys and all the money I have on me. We call World Airways and drive down for a stand-by ticket, the cheapest is at $125. Paul J. comes with us. We buy one round-trip stand-by.

We go home to eat dinner. I fry up the rest of the frozen halibut and we watch *Gone with the Wind*, a true classic, but have to go back to the airport before it ends. We leave Paul there, since he wants to finish the film. Richard and I arrive by 11 p.m. and check in with stand-by. It's nerve-racking—like waiting to win a lottery. So many people, so many stand-bys. My heart beats fast. I think good thoughts and so does Richard. I push myself in front to see them pull the name Bright from the tickets. We made it. I kiss him goodbye. We were not hurt, and that's what really matters, not the stuff. Let me try to not forget that. Oh, Lord.

Monday, March 23rd

After about three hours of sleep I wake up at 6 a.m. Kukums bit me last night when the light went out. I forgot to write on Friday that I had a terrible feeling about the apartment, that something had happened. I had woken up in the morning and couldn't shake it for about thirty minutes. Didn't mention it 'cause I thought it was silly and negative.

Go to work on Stage 16—the Oscar scene. A bit tired and worried about the rest of the apartment. I ask Mauri to call me the moment Richard calls. It's 11:15 a.m. our time, 2:15 p.m. in New York. Richard still hasn't called. I'm worried now about him. When stressed he tends to turn to drugs. So, I try to put all the anxiety and worry into the work—Carol Ann has the same worry and anxiety about who's going to win the Oscar—but I can't bear it and finally call. No answer at New York home. I call information and get the number of Howard Rollins, my dear neighbor, and call him. Howard is there—and so is Richard. Everything's okay, except for the T.V. and a few small items.

In the afternoon, Faye tells me today is Joan Crawford's birthday, and adds she's just got her motor running and wishes she could do this morning all over again. She says she just couldn't get started this morning. She says her son, Liam, has the flu. Her makeup man, Lee, is sick, too, but working. Faye says a couple of times, "Come on, let's get on with it, let's quit wasting time." She says that they're so slow and keep us waiting after calling us to set. I don't think they realize the energy an actor uses up—I tell Faye that, she agrees.

Mara is a little rowdy today. Jeremy is not concentrating, as well. He doesn't follow directions well, he doesn't listen, they have to tell him several times, but he is so young and so very sweet. I tell Frank P. about the burglary and he says, "At least you have each other and that's what really counts. We put too much into the material." Vivienne gives me a piece of her chicken she cooked and Hilda comes in on lunch hour to give me a manicure.

I have ten minutes to lie down. I fortify myself with coffee and cookies in the late afternoon. I ask Faye where Terry is. She says business meetings. She says she got a lovely letter from Paul Mann (one of my acting teachers, as well as Faye's, when she was with the Lincoln Center Repertory Theater under Elia Kazan). It's about Barbara Loden (Kazan's deceased wife and actress) and what she said to him about what Faye had said at the Tony Awards. (I wish I had remembered to write down what it said—though I do recall that I didn't want to tell Faye what Barbara had said about her when Faye was understudying Barbara in "After the Fall," Arthur Miller's famous play about Marilyn Monroe, for which Barbara had gotten fantastic recognition as the Monroe character. She said that Faye was always up in the rafters screwing somebody and wondered if she ever paid attention to what was going on with the performance that she was supposed to be understudying.)

I wrote Katja Raganelli (German director and documentarian) yesterday to send me her script and I will give it to Faye for the film she wants to make. She had asked me if I would do that. I won't tell Faye until it arrives.

One of the extras steps out to talk to Faye and introduce himself and remind her that he danced near her in *Evita* and carries on a conversation, though it's late and Faye's tired. I can see where being a star can wear and tear. We do Faye's close-ups at the end—this is the first time that Faye has done that and is only doing it because the children had to be released first. I try to be there, be involved and let that move me. After I've talked myself into involvement, let it affect me, not act it. It's a real simple key, I think, yet so hard to do. Must continue along these lines and test more in the days ahead.

Tonight Paul J. calls to offer assistance and Richard calls to let me know he changed the tumblers in the locks. I play with Kukums for over an hour. He bites me then later cuddles with me. I miss Richard, and yet I am glad he is not here. I am relieved. I am happy that he is in New York and that he's there taking care of the apartment. It's worth not having that anxiety for two months.

(I think because of the apartment drama, I forgot to journal how Irene Sharaff walked off the film. I ran into her while I was pacing, stressed, around the Paramount lot and she told me how upset she was about Faye changing her costume designs, including the one for that scene. Ms. Sharaff—winner of five Academy Awards for Best Costume Design—had a beautiful, bespoke cashmere robe made in white for Faye, but now Faye was listening to Bernadene (Faye's wardrobe assistant) and another minor person and wearing totally inappropriate, frilly things that Joan never would have worn. Ms. Sharaff said that she had never in her entire career walked off a set, but she was walking now, and not stopping until she was on a flight back to New York. I told her I was sorry that she was leaving and she wished me a lot of luck, said I and the rest of the company would need it—"I have never in my whole career been treated as badly by anyone as by this drug addict. You have to throw a piece of meat into her dressing room before you go in there." I walked her to the gate and watched her walk away, then went to my trailer with heart pangs.)

Tuesday, March 24th

Get up at 6 a.m., play with Kukums until 6:30. Report to work at 7. Pool scene today. Get ready. Cold, so Paul, the D.P., gives me his jacket. I take pictures of Faye and Frank P. rehearsing, and Faye looks up, furious at who's photographing, then says, "Oh, it's Rutanya." I decide not to push it and upset her. Faye and Steve and Mara do their scene and I'm on the side that was never on camera until Steve leaves. I chose to knit rather than read. Worked on a little blue baby sweater.

I haven't shot yet when we break for lunch. Terrible food lately. Even Frank Y. had mentioned the lunches have really gone downhill. Have lunch at the table with Amy and David Koontz, who are talking with Teresa about her new relationship with the man she's living with. The subject shifts to violence and guns. I mention that I wouldn't hesitate to shoot someone who came into my home intending me harm. David says, "You and Christina would really get along. She knows how to use a gun, learned after she was confronted at home by a knife wielding crazy." That exchange clears Teresa and Amy quickly. David says I shocked them away.

Wait around on the set some more. Bruce, the P.R. man, interviews me for a half an hour. See Frank Y. on the grass, playing poker with Jonathan, his young assistant. Terry O'Neill's there, too. I take some photos—currently, Jonathan owes Frank seven-hundred-and-eighty-thousand dollars. Jonathan says you own my house, my car, my mother. Frank says you can keep your mother. I tell Frank that I told Bruce I was a member of the Frank Yablans Repertory Company. He says absolutely. Terry and I speak about swimming. He says he can only swim with his head under water—he doesn't breathe and just the power gets him through the pool. Earlier, apparently Mara had a problem diving because she kept her weight all in her ass, instead of throwing it forward—Frank P. worked with her and so did Victoria, who did the swimming for Faye.

They get me in the shot finally around 5 p.m., after a big hurry up and wait this morning. (As Steve leaves, you see me knitting.) Frank Y. tells me this is Steve's final day. I go up afterward to say how much I have enjoyed working with him. He says Ina Bernstein at ABC is a big fan of mine, she's in casting. I tell Steve I will send him photos of him and the Franks that I took, then I have Bruce take one of all of us, though I feel bad after because I said, "Just me and Frank and Frank."

Frank P. said, "Don't you want Steve in this one?"

I said "Yes, of course," but I had been negligent and worried that I hurt Steve's feelings.

Wrap. Go pick up Fotomat film and then to the drug store. Head home and get mail and open it. Kukums bites me 'cause I didn't play with him right away. He needs attention, he's a living being—I think he was upset about being alone so much today. I play with him throughout the evening. He snuggles with me a little and sleeps on my lap. I had cramps all day today. Watch *Gone with the Wind*, part two. Richard calls. Coming back Thursday. Tired. Go to sleep late. Midnight and Kukums still wants to play, jumping on the bed to attack me. I give him a swat with my pillow. I don't want him to get in the habit of attacking me, especially when I'm sleeping. He doesn't sleep in the bedroom with me tonight. He's pouting.

Wednesday, March 25th

Up at 6 a.m. Play with Kukums for twenty minutes and then call Master Card to straighten out our account, which somehow has been deactivated. Spend a while on the phone with idiots—have to work this out when I come home, but they say they are re-instating our account as of tomorrow.

I'm late. Rush and rush to get out and into makeup and hair, but they're doing a birthday party close-up of Faye, so I won't work for hours. Lunch is half an hour. I eat with a man named Richard from the hair department and Teresa. Richard points out that the doctor who owns the location, his wife, mother and father are all eating for free down at our long table. Richard says how much he hates doctors' wives—he worked at a shop in New York and doctors' wives were the worst. She needs a touch up and her roots are showing under blonde hair. I sit around some more then go to my trailer and lie down. No one calls me, so I just sit in the background and knit a little.

Steve Forrest is back today for a pick-up shot. I cancel dinner with Froma because of cramps and fatigue. We lose light fast after 5 p.m. and we don't get coverage on the shots with Faye and Mara, so we'll have to come back. There's a big meeting with Frank and Frank and the staff. I hear them. They say we'll shoot the death mortuary scene tomorrow. I decide I better talk to Frank P. about the line I want to add: "Oh my friend, why did you go before me." So, I tell him, and he says he wants to think about it. He says it may be too maudlin. I don't say anything more, because I realize the timing is bad with all the pressures and changes, but I want to fight for that line.

They change my call to 6:30 a.m. tomorrow to finish the scene. Then as I'm getting dressed, Bob changes my call to hold—they'll do the pick-up on the Friday and also the mortuary scene Friday. Wow, that's a lot. Tomorrow they'll do the reading of the will. I think I should be at the will reading and so does Bob, so I go to ask Frank P., but he's in a meeting again with Frank Y. in his trailer. I ask if I'm in the will scene, he says no. I decide to drop it. It doesn't really matter. I tell Michael, the assistant director, I won't be there tomorrow. He thinks I should be.

Friday will be a long day. I hope they don't sacrifice coverage, meaning me, because Faye will get covered, dead or not. I'll fight for it on Friday. I'm happy about overtime, though.

Oh, today Faye and I read the horoscopes in *Cosmopolitan*, a real junk magazine—Teresa and I had a real laugh about some of the story garbage. Faye is a Capricorn. She had a good horoscope. I also told her about our fishing. She said she likes to fish as well.

I go home. The script is there from my German filmmaker friends, Katja and Konrad. It's called *The Yellow Wallpaper* by Charlotte Perkins Gilman. Katja adapted it. I play with Kukums and read it.

Thursday, March 26th

Awoken at 6 a.m. by Kukums, my little alarm clock. I had to swat at him with a pillow after he knocked down all my curlers. He then let me sleep till 9:30. I got up feeling very tense. All day there's a slight headache, tension in shoulders and neck—I think it's nerves about doing the funeral scene. I want to be so good. I've got to just get back to doing the work and not want people to like me and think I'm good. I've just got to do the work.

I go out to do errands, bring cleaning back, go pick up a check at the agency. There's letter there from a lady in Tennessee asking for my autograph—she "collects autographs from famous people," which makes me smile. It's a sweet compliment.

See Warren Miller outside the agency. He had just gone to apply for a chauffeur job, but didn't know if he could say yes, sir. I tell him to go to a temp agency as well. He says that's a good idea, as Unemployment just canceled his extension and he's got to get something right away 'cause the money for his screenplay won't come in for a while. Then I go food shopping at Quinn's, come home, and take Kukums out for a walk, when it starts raining, so we go back and the phone rings—Richard is coming in tonight. He went to the airport and got the seat for stand-by. I mention Jane had called from Al Pacino's office and I had told her to call New York. I take a nap with Kukums. Paul Jenkins and Harrison Starr call—I tell Harrison to call Robin for Frank Y.'s okay to visit the set.

I decide to stay home for the evening. I feel anxious—call for work tomorrow 6:45 a.m. Froma calls. Watch T.V. Go to pick up Richard at airport 11:55 p.m. Take Kukums. Richard is surprised that Kukums is there. It is good to see him, but I am quickly feeling stressed again. Go to sleep at 2.

Friday, March 27th

Up at 5:30 a.m, have to be at the Van Ness Gate at 6:45. Play with Kukums a bit. Leave Richard sleeping, he's had a rough three days. I arrive at the gate and park the car. There's a Cadillac waiting to take me to the Beverly Glen location. I try to save my strength. It's going to be a long day and one I'm dreading a bit—the funeral sequence when we move to the mortuary location. It's going to be emotionally demanding. Hope I'm up to it.

They do me up for the '40s look to say, "On your mark, get set, go!" for the pool race that Faye and Mara have. Only today, there is no one in the pool. I have to try and imagine it all. They do two shots of me saying it at both ends of the pool. Three takes. Frank wanted it not to be so casual, that it was symbolic—especially the line "on your marks," for this race symbolizes the relationship of these two women throughout their lives. I finally get it the way he wanted it on the third take, then they send me to go get into my old age makeup.

Diana is being done for her first scene with Faye at the funeral home. She looks very elegant in her black suit, with a blonde wig and black hat. Someone asks her as we go to get water if she's enjoyed working on this film and she says, "Not especially." Her candor surprises me. I meet the actor who plays the grown up Christopher, Xander Berkeley, and the actor that plays David,

Robert Harper.

Go back to makeup. Charlie is making up Steve Forrest, who's back again for another take. We kid him about not being able to get rid of him. He is happy about Carol Burnett winning her suit against *National Enquirer*. He says they had tried to get information on him about the success of his long marriage and he had refused to talk with them or have them on the set of *S.W.A.T.*, when he was starring on the show.

After they finish Steve, Charlie starts putting on my old age makeup. About a half-hour into the makeup, they decide they need me to match the shot from the other day when I sat there and knitted. Charlie says he can't take the makeup off and then put it on again—I would have no skin left. So, they decide to strike my sitting there. Now I'll appear at the pool from out of nowhere. Hurry up, hurry up, and then they make mistakes. It's silly to rush so. I know they're under pressure. Oh well, let it go and think about the important scene at the funeral parlor.

It's now about 12:30 and they decide to move us to the other location. We get there around 1:10 and have lunch 1:15 to 1:45, then back to makeup. We finish in another hour and Diana and Faye are still doing their scene. I go to the set and see Faye in the coffin, and I get choked up with tears and emotion. I tell Frank Perry all I really need is just to see Faye lying there, that will really get me going. I really don't need a line. They like my makeup. I tell them to tell Charlie, he deserves the credit. The makeup is better today than at the test, it's softer. I tell Charlie to look out for me and make sure they light me right. He says he will. He says he's pretty quiet generally, but he'll speak up and fight when he has to.

I decide against the hat they had picked out for me. It does not sit right on my head. It's too small with my wig, which they didn't factor in. The lady doesn't have any more hats with her and when she stretches it out it still doesn't fit. I really need a hat, but there isn't one. Irene Sharaff would have a fit. I have to forget about the hat. The wig looks good.

I go sit in the funeral parlor to get the feel of it. It's a nice, old place—a real funeral parlor, though I understand it's been closed down. Too near the freeway now. Lots of oak, painted over oak, oak staircase, and lots of flower bouquets on the set. Joan would have liked it.

I stay there a while and decide I better save my strength, so I go lie down in my trailer. About an hour goes by and they come and get me for the blocking and rehearsal. I go to the viewing room with the coffin, but there is no Faye inside, just a Polaroid picture of her. I stupidly expected Faye to stay in the coffin for me. It seems that Faye doesn't want to stay in the coffin anymore. Faye is on her way home. But when did she ever stay for my close-ups? Never! It's always the script person who reads her lines, or the director. Then Frank decides we have no time left to do this shot. They have spent hours and hours shooting Faye in the coffin—they have no time to shoot my scene. I have been cut from that scene, where I say goodbye to Faye in the coffin, the one I have been preparing for all day. Carol Ann does not have a farewell with Joan? Are they kidding?! I'm upset. They are rushing quickly on to the Carol Ann and Christina scene and do all of Diana's stuff first, then I come in—but it's being shot from my back! Not on my face! Carol Ann gets screwed! Again! I do want to get the right emotion in my voice and give something. And I do. But I have to save myself for my close-up, too. Diana cries a lot. She does well, she's a weeper. To her, acting is crying. Then they change the camera angles and the shoot the mortuary man and his speech. How about Carol Ann? I'm frustrated. I wish I wasn't always the last one to get close-ups.

Frank Y. leaves the set around 7, he isn't feeling well. Frank P. gets upset over something about 7:30. I don't want to know what, because I don't want my concentration affected. It turns out to be that his secretary, Robin, never showed up because she didn't want to come to a mortuary, since her grandma had apparently died eight months before and she would be too upset. Frank had been expecting her since noon and Mauri had given Frank the message about 7:30 p.m., not knowing anything. Frank is furious with Robin. When the mortician actor asks Frank about acting and his lines at one point, Frank says he doesn't want acting now, he just wants to move people around—he would be very upset if he sees acting. He says that's one thing he learned from John Frankenheimer. I say what's that? He says how to move bodies around. I have to remember that too: Save everything for when the camera's on. Save all the energy for when it counts. Important lesson. We're not endless in energy. We only have so much to give at the right time.

At one point, I sit with Frank P. on the couch. I touch his cheek with my hand—tears swell into his eyes. I don't know what that was all about. Maybe tenderness really moves him. He is under a lot of pressure today and I think he's handled it very well. Frank tells Michael, the A.D., about the hundred-thousand dollar funeral in '77 at Campbell's Funeral Home in Manhattan for Sue Kaufman (author of *Diary of a Mad Housewife*, the film adaptation of which became one of his early hits), "When she committed suicide" (as opposed to the accepted narrative of a long illness). I don't want to hear it. My scene is next. I only want to think about Joan and my life without her. I shut myself off and walk away. Later, I come back and sit on the couch again. Michael comes and sits down beside me and says wow about the stuff he'd just heard from Frank. I say I don't want to hear it.

It's around 8 p.m., I feel drained. My emotions that seemed so full just a few hours ago feel sapped. Finally, it comes time for me. It must be 8:30. Right before my take Teresa says, "Here goes 'One Take' Alda." I resent it. I must not let myself get rushed because the crew is tired and they all want to go home. Must not feel rushed. Take my time! Important!

Just before I enter, Frank P. surprises me with the Polaroid of Faye in her coffin. I take it out the door with me. It gets me. I just look at the photo and say, "My poor baby, my poor baby, my baby's gone," and that triggers it for me. I come in very full. It's an excellent scene and I feel the work is good. Diana says it's wonderful. There seems to be a problem with Diana blocking me through some of it. Frank wants to go for another. I say okay. There is talking outside. I tell them to shhhhh. My concentration is not full. I feel I should take more time, but everyone's rushing. I'm in the middle of the second take and I realize it's not as full or good as the first one. Still good but not as good. Frank says that's it, he wants to save it for the two-shot of us in profile. I ask for another take on me. He says no. He wants to save me for the two shot. He says he got it on the first take, the good one. I say I thought you said it was blocked. He says only a small part of it blocked one of my eyes, it was good. I have to believe him. I hope he's telling me the truth. So, I save it for the two-shot, which goes well for both of us. Frank says that's it, he has it. Frank asks me for the Polaroid back. Darn. I wish I could keep it. No, he says, he needs it back.

I ask, "Could we do one more take?"

"No, I have it, brilliant work. Excellent, wonderful work." Then he goes off to praise Diana. I feel again like a second banana, I have to fight that. He's pampering Diana now. He wishes her good luck at the Oscars. His priorities are there. She's the Oscar contender.

The actor who plays David, Robert Harper, comes up to me and introduces himself. He says my scene was very nicely done. Jan, from hair, is making fun of Faye because she wanted everyone out when she prepared for her scene in the coffin. They don't understand—that was the one time she was entitled to the Clear Away Club. John, Frank's driver, comes up to me as I'm walking to my trailer to tell me how much he enjoyed watching me and my work. I'm taken aback a bit. I realize he's very sincere. I say I didn't even know he was there. He walks me to the trailer and says "I'll get you some more film next week, Rutanya"—he has given me some 35-millimeter film before for my camera. This is very sweet of him.

I go in and tear my clothes off and don't even hang them up for the first time. I'm exhausted. (I remember feeling like I had just attended my own funeral). I want some of the flower arrangements—they're all grabbing them. I go in and ask Bob Doherty, the second assistant director, for some. He gets me a heavy basket of beautiful red carnations with the Maryland Fan Club banner on them. I take them to the makeup trailer.

Charlie puts a hot towel on my face, and then peels most of the stuff off. The neck hurts the most—that is the biggest appliance. He hot towels it again, doesn't hurt as much as the last time. We finish and I thank him for staying and helping me. Jan is there too. She takes the wig. Charlie says, "Oh, I really didn't want to go dancing tonight, anyway." We finish and all rush to the Cadillac, which takes us back to the parking lot at Paramount. I put the flowers in the back seat and it's now 9:45 p.m. We finished at the set at 9:05. Lots of overtime.

As I drive back to the Marmont, I hope Richard is there waiting for me. It seems like forever getting back. Traffic is awful. I carry the flowers and myself upstairs. He is there. It's good to snuggle and be held. I need that. Around 11 p.m., Richard goes out to be with Paul. Oh no, oh boy, drugs! I wash up and hit the pillow at midnight.

Saturday, March 28th

Lunch with actor friend Alan Feinstein and Lana Wood, Natalie Wood's sister, at The Source. Alan and Lana are going together. Alan is studying with Milton Katselas and took pride in telling us he's working on a scene from the play "La Cage aux Folles." Lana is working as a producer's assistant at Universal. She has a little girl, six years old—she keeps asking us if we want her. Somehow I feel she is not kidding. I think there is some desire to be single and free for her. It's a nice lunch, though. Richard catches some girl doing drugs in the bathroom. We pick up the tab and they give us tickets for the Woody Guthrie show at the Solari, which they can't use. The show proves okay, very monotonous, but a one-man show is very courageous.

(Lana didn't know and I didn't tell her that I had met her when she was little with Natalie, who had just finished her big break in the 1956 film *The Searchers* with John Wayne. I was in Arizona, speaking broken English, and had gone to the Hotel Monte Vista having heard that it was actor Jeff Hunter's final day in Flagstaff. He was the sweetest person and took a lot of time walking with me as I showed him around, then back to the hotel, where he introduced me to Natalie, who gave me her autograph. I just remember Lana sitting in the hotel lobby with a huge pout, not speaking to anyone, then just glaring as Natalie made a point of introducing her. She was not having any of it. Then I walked Mr. Hunter to the railroad station and he kissed me on the cheek, which I didn't wash for a whole week. But I didn't feel like sharing this with Lana, because it still meant a lot to me and I felt she really wouldn't have cared.)

Sunday, March 29th

Laundry day. Richard always resents having to do it. Learn that the change machines are out of order after we have put everything in. Richard goes to get some. The laundromat has really gone downhill. Lots of sick types with people scratching their fleas off. Richard brought a burrito and I ask for a bite. After the third bite, he really resents giving it to me. I get mad that he won't share his burrito. He gets mad and leaves me with the laundry. I think that Richard always finds a reason not to do the laundry. When the clothes are in the dryer, he comes back. I'm surprised and glad. If he hadn't, I'd be really mad. We finish and go to Quinn's for groceries, then to Filmex and get our series tickets. Come home. Richard is tired and goes to bed early. I do, too, although I can't fall asleep right away.

Monday, March 30th

Call Diana to wish her good luck at the Oscars. Call Bobby [De Niro] to wish him luck and Richard says break an Oscar. Run into Joe Pesci downstairs and wish him good luck. Go to the bank and then at 1 p.m. break my rule of not seeing rushes, because I'm curious to see how the funeral scene had gone. Take Kukums with us. Richard isn't allowed to see the dailies, so he leaves and I stay with Kukums. Kukums absolutely panics, I've never seen him like this. I can hardly control him. Glad when the dailies are over. Only two of me—a half-figure and a profile shot in the scene. The profiles of me and Diana were wasted, as far as I am concerned. And my one take was good, I just feel cheated on the coverage. I feel they just ran out of time on Friday. They always shoot me last, when everyone is rushing. Should have taken two days on this or at least one whole day. The values are compromised with me. They covered Diana well. I think I'll tell Frank tomorrow. It's upsetting.

After the dailies we take Kukums to the vet. He gets three shots and his anal glands squeezed. Vet says to take him off dry food. He foams at the mouth on the way back and later this evening. We get worried and called the emergency number. But he's settled down—crawled under the couch. I guess he doesn't feel good from all the shots. Go to Filmex to exchange tickets. We are persistent and get it. We pick up photos and come back and watch news of the shooting of President Reagan on T.V. Write some letters. Richard then takes off at 10 p.m. to see Paul J. This is bad news. I know he's going to get drugs. He really doesn't care about my work.

Tuesday, March 31st

Report to makeup at 7 a.m. Frank asks me how I liked the dailies for the funeral scene. I tell him I didn't. I think I could have done more but it was shot at the fifteenth hour and I didn't get the time I needed to prepare. He says I am crazy. It was perfect the first take, that was all he needed. He says it's the most moving scene in the whole film and to believe him that I am confusing the situation we shot under with what was on film—that I should take pride in and find satisfaction with what I've accomplished and not be so critical. He also says he couldn't go in for a close-up because of the makeup—it would show. I'm glad I spoke to him. He seems sincere. But I do feel second-class, sometimes.

At 1 p.m., my agent Kendall meets Richard and me for lunch at Oblatt's. She says she wouldn't have recognized me with the hair, I look so different. She speaks of the difficulties now of people not committing themselves because of the possibility of a strike. Very, very slow. We finish and I take Kendall for a tour of the set. Richard leaves. I have Kendall come to hair and makeup. She tells me she is living with a guy, an unemployed actor, for the first time ever—how she's not telling her mother, who would be shocked, and of the difficulties of two people living in a small space. I ask Frank and Frank to meet my agent. They look stone-faced. I say she's that good-looking blonde over there. They both light up and I bring her over. Frank P. says you have a very talented client, but I fear Kendall misses it because she is talking to Frank Y. It's a nice two minute social, then they were ready to resume shooting. Kendall leaves.

The fan club scene: When I suggest to Frank that I fix something on Faye before the photographers shoot her, he thinks that is a most creative touch. I'm barely in the shot though, so all the care that I show for Joan? Wasted, not shown. Also, the shot at the end of the day around 5:30 p.m., when Faye comes down the stairs to greet the fans and we all look up? Wasted.

I come home to find a note that Richard is at Paul J.'s. Oh, no. Richard comes home around 6:30 and I watch the Oscars while he takes a bath. We go to sleep around 10:30.

Wednesday, April 1st

Up at 6 a.m. Rose Garden scene. They get me ready. Vivienne has a bad flu. I do a quick shot walking both kids in. Then they don't use me again until 5:15 p.m. "Hurry, hurry, we lose the kids in fifteen minutes. Hurry up!" Bad planning. They always wait till right before they lose the kids to use them. They'd been doing Faye all day by herself. Close-ups. Once again, Faye didn't stand-in for us for the reaction to cutting the tree. When has she ever! I'm disappointed. One take, then another take with all of us and the fallen tree—that was it. I feel badly used again. (By the way, it was Frank Perry—with his visible hands—who chopped the little tree down. Faye wasn't strong enough to do it.)

Charlie says he went to bed the other night and woke up cursing. If he had to do it again, he wouldn't do this film. He says after all the work he'd done on the old age, they hadn't bothered to shoot it right. They'd shot it in the fourteenth hour, when all the crew wanted to go home. He says he doesn't like Frank P. as a director and won't work with him again. He also says he'll never work again where he's shuttled off to another room. He is used to being behind the camera, and if an actress can't work with the crew there then she shouldn't be acting (meaning Faye, who as the president of the Clear Away Club, cleared her sight lines all day long today). I tell Charlie I spoke to Frank P. about the funeral scene and we didn't get a close-up, contrary to what he thought. Charlie says, "I never promised you a rose garden, but you're getting a thorny one."

Michael Daves comes up to me and asks what is Faye wearing, a net skirt or what? I say a net. The bottom-half looks like a ballet dancer, the top-half a gold lamé top. And this outfit, in the rose garden? Ms. Sharaff would be having a reaction right now! I'm sure this costume has been changed by Faye, as Ms. Sharaff would never have designed it.

I bought *The Troll Book* for Jeremy. He really likes it and brought it to school to show his teacher and he and Mara take turns reading it. His father comes up and thanks me for it and for being so nice to him. We wish each other good luck. Mara tells me how much she likes me in front of Frank P. "You are the best maid I've ever worked with." Frank says Mara's really grown in the last three months and has become more mature and a better actress, more real. Frank also says that I am much more than a maid, I have talent.

I've made arrangements to shoot headshots tomorrow with Ralph Nelson. Marshall's leaving for *Annie* (1982). People are abandoning ship, looking for their next job. Kathy Blondell (Faye's hairstylist) says she'd give him a surprise cake on Friday.

Richard comes and picks me up. Earlier he met me for lunch. I speak to Denise (my New York neighbor) on the phone about a problem they were having with turning the gas on for the building. I tell her to leave a note for Con Ed: We have no pilot light in our apartment and ancient stove. Mark (a downstairs neighbor) calls later and Richard repeats it aloud, basically they're going to call us collect tomorrow to verify everything. Kukums more lively today, but not eating too much of the canned food—wants the dry food.

Thursday, April 2nd

Get ready and put on a beautiful white suit for photo session with Ralph at Paramount. Get there around 1:30 p.m. On my way in, with the suit and rollers and no makeup, I run into Frank Y., who says he loves the outfit and gives me a big hug and introduces me to Roger Ebert.

Charlie does my makeup during his lunch hour. They had not gotten their first shot till 1:15. Something about how the set—Joan and Al Steele's N.Y. apartment—had been built without space for the lights and they had to spend the entire morning reworking it. Richie does my hair. Vivienne says I look like Venus in Botticelli's Primavera and later Charlie says I look like Vivien Leigh.

It is cold and windy. We go outdoors and shoot a roll of film, white suit on against the white background. As I was standing there someone shouts as he drives by, "Hello gorgeous!" Bob and Louis, the A.D., do a double-take. I don't want to go to the stage because I don't want to upset Faye in any way.

I finish and call Richard. He picks me up and I decide to take a chance and go see Cis Corman (casting director who cast me in *The Deer Hunter*), seeing as I look so great. She is casting at the Chateau

Marmont (for Marty Scorsese's *The King of Comedy* with Jerry Lewis and Bobby). On my way in to see Cis, Gale, her assistant, signals at the window not to come in that she will call me on the phone. I head back upstairs. She calls and says they were taping and it would have upset everything because they were working with a girl who was a non-actress. She says to call tomorrow at 9:15 a.m. Cis is free for a half-hour then. Damn.

Friday, April 3rd

Get up at 8:30 a.m. and get ready to see Cis. Hold off taking my rollers out till the last minute. Cis says to call back in two, which I do, as she is having a tough time getting Marty in today. Richard and I dress up and I wear my white suit and we head to her bungalow. It is cold and damp. Cis says she loves Marty but she has to be like a mother to him. He has asthma and is having a tough time with another attack. They are pushing everyone back a half-hour with appointments. Cis thinks it was awful that the Directors Guild didn't give their award to Marty (for his 1980 film *Raging Bull*). She told him the Academy would never give him the Oscar, but it was a shame the Directors didn't. She says he got letters from all over the world—from Kurosawa and from Europe—they think he's a genius. She says that after one-and-a-half hours of working with an actor on videotape, Marty is pooped out. She doesn't know how he gets through a whole film, he just gives so much.

They got a nasty letter from an agent for some actress, who used to be a friend, complaining how badly she'd been treated—how nasty they'd all been to her. That really hurt Cis, I could see she was really upset by the letter. Cis also says there was a line in the script they're doing now that she's going to use: "They have complete faith in my judgment."

We talked about what husbands do when they're staying with wives. How her husband drives her and picks up shopping, et cetera. Richard says he does the same. Cis says they are looking for someone really strange for the girl. I say you don't know how strange I really am and if they don't find anyone, have me in for a reading. She says she will. She says that Marty had originally wanted someone specific, but upon seeing her again in L.A. changed his mind. Cis says she wants to go home to New York.

Before we go, Richard helps give directions to some guy who comes in to read. Cis says she just loves Richard.

Richard goes to take Paul somewhere. I shower and wash my hair. Afterward I take a nap for a half-hour with Kukums. They call to make sure I'll be in at 4 p.m. for the close-up shot on my opening scene. It seems they have to change a line because there is no accident now, so my line doesn't make sense. They're not doing the ice skating sequence. Too expensive. (They were going to recreate a scene from Joan Crawford's *The Ice Follies of 1939*, just as they reference *Mildred Pierce*. In film, time wasted can cost a production more than just money.)

Richard takes me to the studio, to Stage 31, and I head to makeup and hair. Vivienne is there, even though she is still sick. They finished yesterday's shooting today. So we're behind again a few hours. As Vivienne does my hair, Kathy (Faye's hairstylist) is doing Faye's wig. On Kathy's way out, Vivienne says, "Oh, my baby." I say what? She says never mind, but afterward says she is just upset about how Kathy had made a mess of "her baby," the beautiful wig that I first saw, that Kathy doesn't know how to do wigs. Vivienne says she and Jan could have really made a name for themselves on this film, if they'd have left them alone, but Kathy has ruined all the wigs. She repeats how Faye had wanted Kathy because she had done Goldie Hawn's hair in *Private Benjamin* and Faye liked her hair and wanted that look. But this is the '30s and the '40s, not the '80s. I ask, didn't Faye know that Kathy can't do wigs? She says well lately she's figured it out and that's why Faye and Kathy barely speak to each other. Jan says they have left it alone after Faye came in to the trailer screaming at Vivienne about how nobody cuts her wigs except Kathy. Vivienne says Faye later apologized at a dailies screening. I remember when she said "You were right Viv—they're the most beautiful wigs I've ever seen." Vivienne says the real Crawford wouldn't be caught in hair like that, she was so elegant and meticulous. Charlie doesn't think Faye is a good actress. He thinks she's good in some scenes, but too much screaming. Vivienne agrees. Vivienne says the real Joan was also never so rude and nasty as Faye. I listen. I don't say much.

I go on the set. They're finishing up Faye who is having her makeup done. Bruce, the P.R. man, somehow has the makeup man's role. Faye seems distant and down. I wonder right away if she's mad at me for some reason. Did she overhear some conversations in the trailer? I've been keeping my mouth shut—just let me keep it shut through this film, please.

Later, I talk to Lee, Faye's personal makeup man. They've been working since 7 a.m. She's had the old age makeup on since this morning and Lee says it is really hard on her skin. Duhhhhh, tell me about it. Her skin is so thin, he says, from all the weight loss and weight gain. I say I didn't know she had a weight problem. He says she's gained ten pounds since this film has started—he says he left her for two weeks during *The Champ* (1979) and when he came back she had gained twenty pounds, she just sat in the motel and ate. He had to take her to a weight farm for a week to lose some of it.

He also says this is his eleventh film with her, and this is the toughest. She's down because Terry keeps telling her at night that she can't act, she's no good. I am shocked! How can he do that? An actress's ego is so fragile. He says Terry is just using her to get ahead and he thinks she may be getting wise to that. I asked earlier if she was pregnant during *The Champ* and Lee said no. I ask doesn't their baby mean anything to Terry? Silence.

I watch her as she finishes her inserts, walking across the stage. She walks marvelously. They do a very wide shot. Faye wasn't wearing makeup but her face won't show. After they finish with Faye, I go up to her and hug her. She says, "Would you mind terribly if I didn't stay?" Is she delusional, when did she ever once? I could see she was drained. But you know what? So am I, and I'm always the last one to be filmed, by myself, with the script person pretending to be Joan.

I say "I'll miss you, of course, but I'll pretend you're there." She smiles and hugs me. I tell her she was marvelous, just the way she walked across the stage. She brightened and smiled a thank you. I feel sorry for her at this moment. But just for a moment, because she got out of not being my acting partner again. It's such bullshit for an actor to never be there for their scene partner.

Crap, Frank P. says he is tired, that he is really tired. He says he feels like a sow with twenty-four tits—everyone suckling and wanting more. We set up for our scene. I get a present from Frank and Frank, a blue cardigan *Mommie Dearest* sweater (which I later gave to an adoring fan who worked at The Gap on Broadway, who was elated). I would rather have gotten another little gold chain. I thank Frank and Frank.

We do the shot. The obnoxious extra is there again. He is with a new woman extra. Two takes, that's it. I picture Barbara Loden when I say to Joan, "How brave and wonderful you are." I say it to Barbara even though it is meant for Faye. The "eighteen hour day line" is for Faye, though. I hope they both come through.

We finish at 8:30 p.m. I change. There is Chinese food and beer. I wait for Richard. It is 9:20. They are closing the stage. I leave with Mauri to go back to the office. We leave word for Richard. We find each other around 9:40. We are both angry.

Saturday, April 4th

Meet Denise Sickinger, my friend, at Filmex. She's getting married April 16th, on her birthday, in New York. We're invited but can't be there. See two new films: the Czechoslovakian *Love Between the Raindrops* and the French *La Banquière*.

Sunday, April 5th

Meet Ellen Whitman and her love Sam at Filmex. See the Russian film *The Mirror*. Go out for Japanese food afterward.

Monday, April 6th

Call Katja, who is in New York. Speak of the film and her wanting an August start for filming in Ireland. She's sending me a script and one for Faye. Turns out she had sent me the short story before and not the script, which she's finally finished. She says she showed some of her documentary of Barbara Loden to Elia Kazan and that he was very upset by it, but pleased. Elia also seemed pleased to see that Barbara and I share a scene, where she directs me.

Tuesday, April 7th

Sleep. Tired in afternoon. Go to the Garfields' for dinner. Watch part of *Masada*.

Wednesday, April 8th

Work at 7 a.m. at Van Ness Gate at Paramount. The people mover moves me to the Beverly Hilton Hotel for the Las Vegas wedding sequence. I have my middle age makeup on and a beautiful gray taffeta wedding party dress. This is the dress Ms. Sharaff mentioned was by a famous French designer when we were having wardrobe fittings at the beginning of the film. It is gorgeous and fits me perfectly. I have a cute hat on and I look so good. Faye is in a beautiful pink satin dress that buttons down the front with an orchid corsage. Harry Goz was there as Al Steele, as well as about twenty-five extras. One lady comments that I have the smallest waist. Faye overhears this and gives me a look. They have a room for me to wait in: Room 111 at the hotel across the pool from the shooting room. I offer it to Teresa to share with me so she can sleep. She is sick. Soon members of the Clear Away Club join us, who didn't have another space to hold their regularly scheduled meeting.

Frank P. comes by and says they will not use me in the wedding scene. What! How can you not have Carol Ann at the wedding? "You look too good, Rutanya," Frank says. "I told you this at the beginning, you can't look good. I have no control over this."

"But Frank," I stammer, "This costume was approved in the test shots, I mean I can justify Christina not being there, if she is in school or in New York, although I think she should have been there too. But Carol Ann! She should be making sure the photographers get really good shots, and she could be giving last-minute photos to sign, as Joan was always signing her eight-by-tens, and she should be making sure Joan looks good. There are twenty-five strangers there who have never been seen in the film. They don't mean anything."

"It's out of my hands, Faye doesn't want it," Frank says, and quickly leaves. Incredible! Frank is so afraid of Faye. *He's* afraid of being fired by her!

Come home around 6 p.m. Richard is strange. I think he's taken drugs. His face is ashen. I ask him, he says no. He is very upset and depressed. I have to learn to tell the difference. I think I know now. He is upset over a rejection with a casting woman at Universal—that maybe he was blackballed because of the incident with Sheriff Lobo. (That was when he was hired to do a part, and then they changed the part to a horse killer. Richard would never have accepted that role on principle, and told them he wasn't going to do it, as that was not the part he was cast for. They said they would blackball him. He quit anyway.)

Forgot to mention that Faye got a cortisone shot in the hip. She's apparently been in real bad pain since the swimming pool scene, and the Rose Garden scene kicked it up. A doctor came to the set and gave it to her. I wish I could have given her the shot! Bernadene held her hand. I have a feeling they now want to rush the movie and get it over with because they don't want any delays and are scared about Faye getting sick.

Thursday, April 9th

7 a.m. call at Veterans Memorial Hospital. I have anxiety about being late. My own anxiety. Put on old age makeup again. Faye looks very elegant in an all purple outfit, including purple high heeled boots, which must have cost a fortune, all butter leather. I am waiting when the actor who is playing the doctor gets dismissed to go home. They've cut out his part. He still gets paid, but I feel so bad for him. I identify with him. What a disappointment. Faye has confiscated the line the doctor was supposed to say that Christina is okay and that the doctor said it was a benign tumor. Okay. Another line for Faye, while the rest of us get cut and cut!

I just sit there and wait with her on the opening shot, and then the actress playing the woman producer comes in and it's a scene with those two. Since the doctor was dismissed, now I have to change my acting choice. No longer worried about what is wrong with Christina. We've been told she'll be okay—in my imagination I see the doctor telling us and I repeat the lines in my head of what he would have said—and now we're waiting to tell the producer. I look for something that people do while waiting. I decide on just looking through a magazine, but not really reading, just to pass time.

Faye asks about Richard. I say he'd had a very bad night last night. She asks why and I mention being rejected, but more that it was the way they did it.

She says, "Yes, they can be so cruel sometimes." Yeah! I know!

I say Richard is thinking about giving up acting.

"So am I," she says. "It's always the talented people who get hurt the most."

Faye tells me I look like a little old lady. I'm sure that makes her happy. I tell her she looks so elegant. She says she is supposed to look like that. She says it is weird having old-age makeup on. I agree.

We finish the shot quickly. The girl playing the producer has trouble hitting her marks. They don't do any coverage on me. Once more, Carol Ann is screwed! I tell Charlie that. He says "I noticed. It's sure been a waste of time and effort." I am disappointed. Again! Hopefully I'll get coverage in on my scene with Faye and Diana in my old-age look next week. I wrap at 11:30 a.m. and get ready to go.

Diana is in the makeup trailer when I get my makeup off. She doesn't say anything. Skin really suffers this time, red rash on my face. Everyone else wishes me a good Big Sur weekend—I'll be driving up the coast highway to Big Sur with Richard. I get a photo taken with Faye. Hopefully it'll turn out, the batteries were low.

I come home and Richard isn't there. They've cheated me on my contract to read two weeks of rehearsal and thirteen of photography, that's five thousand dollars lost. Next time I must be more careful signing contracts. Have to let the bad feeling go. Mustn't be poisoned by it. Let it go. I'll get one week at twenty-five hundred extra, anyway. I have to check all overtime. Doesn't seem right—seems like it's been too little.

I go to the studio after Richard comes home to pick up my check. Mauri says they are determined to finish on the 16th, although she doesn't think they can. She thinks they need one more day. She says it may be at the expense of the film. I hope not. She says they're worried about Faye not feeling well, also they don't want to pay holiday pay on the 17th (Good Friday). Mauri gives me her AAA club card to get maps. Head to the bank and get gas. Pick up Richard and take him to MGM for an audition. Go to AAA while he's there and then wait for him. The audition is for Robert Collins of Lorimar for a T.V. pilot. It goes well, apparently. Richard feels a little better today. I always worry when he feels this bad that he'll turn to drugs. Go to Filmex, see the French film, *A Bad Son*, and a Japanese film, *Autumn*. French one—not bad, Japanese one—terrible. Home at midnight.

Friday, April 10th
Get up at 8 a.m. Have to call Bob D. regarding final permission to leave for Big Sur. He finally calls me back at 9:30, says yes. We leave at 10—drop off two sets of tickets with Paul that we can't use tonight for Filmex. We stop by Boyd and Karen's. New litter of kittens were born—all orange like their mother. I bring one to Kukums in the car. He smells it before backing away gently. He's terrific. We stay till 11:45 then leave.

Drive up to Big Sur Lodge. We're there by 5:30. Drive to Carmel and see *American Gigolo* and *The Postman Always Rings Twice*, then drive back. Richard kisses me in the middle of a split Redwood tree we found on the lodge grounds. Wonderful large kissing space in the middle of the tree.

Saturday, April 11th
Have breakfast at 8:30 a.m. at River Inn. Sit by the river. Wonderful male peacock there with his tail-feathers all on display. We drive seventeen miles to Monterey, then up north on Highway 1. Have lunch. I find ten dollars on the floor. We found a dime last night at the theater. Hope this all means good luck. Kukums is with us all day. We take him out for walks.

Drive along the coast. Take photos. Go to Glen Oaks for dessert where we have the best strawberry shortcake. Help out this guy with fan belt problems, has a Volkswagen, by taking him to get a new one. Then we go to the Pfeiffer Beach—wild and woodsy for about two miles before. We sit there for a half-hour. Kukums crawls under my coat. We go for a walk after. Kukums wants to climb trees. We all climb up a giant Redwood that's fallen. Kukums wants to run up all the way.

Take a nap then to Nepenthe restaurant for dinner. It's a famous restaurant in Big Sur with a stunning view. Wait one-and-a-half hours. Terrible food. Then go to Ventana for a cappuccino. Nice place. Another stunning view. It was really our style. Bed by midnight. We write postcards.

Sunday, April 12th

Up early. Get packed. Drive to Lucia, have breakfast at a lovely little place overlooking the sea. Drive down the coast to Hearst Castle—hundreds of people there. We'd have to wait hours, so sadly we pass. Go on to Solvang. Too touristy. Stop by Boyd and Karen's—they weren't home. Show Kukums the cats and the dogs. He's scared but very sweet, not a hostile cat. Run into Boyd and Karen on the way out. Get home and discover my camera missing. Panic with rage against my own stupidity.

Get a call—the camera had been found by Karen in the driveway.

Monday, April 13th

9 a.m. call for fight scene. Jocelyn Brando's there. She is Marlon Brando's sister. We speak a lot. Jocelyn loves to read. She says Marlon's genius is his concentration and his ability to go with his impulses. She says there is nothing else they were both qualified to do. The mother was artistic and an amateur actress and had a drinking problem, but she loved him a lot. She would always put her gentle hand on his forehead when he couldn't sleep. The father was very strict. Jocelyn looks a little like Simone Signoret, the wonderful French actress, whom I adore.

Wait around all day. They didn't get to the fight scene. Dismiss me at 7:10 p.m. I give the scarf that I knitted to Faye. She loves it, says she'll keep it forever. Bernadene said this was a good day for a present for her, she was real low. Faye says she was real down today because of the scene—that she's identified so much with Joan. We exchange addresses. She signs the photos for Andy, Eva, me, and Richard, who earlier took Kukums to the vet. He has tonsillitis. Went to Filmex. Terrible West German film *Palermo oder Wolfsburg* (1980). In bed at 12:30 a.m.

Tuesday, April 14th

Yesterday I forgot to mention that Frank P. greeted me with "Here's my favorite person—do you have a kiss for me?" When I told him we went to Big Sur for the weekend, he said you guys are really something to have the energy to fit it in over the weekend.

Today I am in makeup at 7:10 a.m., then we rehearse the fight scene with the stunt women. I pull Stunt Joan off Stunt Christina. Jocelyn wants to know if we get stunt pay. She is worried about her left arm: She has a plate in it from an auto accident, where she was badly hurt. She lost the lower half of her hair, too, apparently—it got matted from lying in bed in the hospital. It's still long and white, though. (She credited a hairdresser friend for saving the rest of her hair, who would come in for hours and comb and untangle it, strand by strand.)

We finish the stunt scene that we shot without Faye and Diana and now bring in Faye and Diana. Faye has her own idea of the scene. She takes over and makes up lines like, "You never loved me," and "You never were grateful for anything." She wants me to leave her when she puts her hands up. I do, but we already shot the stunt scene, so she's changing the choreography out of sequence. So, I go with my impulse at the end and hug her. Faye knocks me down with her arm. I land on my butt. Frank P. has a very sick smile on his face during the entire fight sequence with Faye and Diana. Jocelyn leaves afterward and we hug each other. She thinks the part will be very good for me. I miss Jocelyn already.

Find out they've cancelled the press party. Faye said she was too tired to do it. The production had hired some models to wear the wonderful clothes that Faye wears as Joan for it. Faye put a stop to it. I guess her contract allows her to do that. I say to Faye, "No one should wear your clothes." She agrees. I am in my Carol Ann mode. I can't believe I am still doing that. (I remember Frank Yablans being really upset by the cancellation. He was a master of propaganda in the best sense, and had arranged for a T.V. crew to film it professionally to drum up attention and anticipation.)

I'm in the trailer changing for inserts of cutting Greg's head from photos when I find out they want to rush everything and finish tomorrow, instead of Thursday. They want me to do two old age makeup changes in the same day. I put my foot down and say no way are they going to do that to my face. Charlie backs me up and says he couldn't do them both on one day, the skin needs some rest, also it would not stay on right. Then they say they would do it all in one old age makeup. But one of the scenes with Faye and me watching T.V. takes place prior to the hospital sequence, so the age wouldn't match. (If you watch my moment in the hospital, you can see the makeup doesn't match. It's a younger makeup. Also, in the scene where Joan and I are watching Christina perform on the soap opera and Joan is signing her eight-by-ten photos on the table, the audience also sees me in my very old-age makeup, though Joan still looks good. Faye was supposed to have had her old-age makeup on, but she had walked in to shoot without it and refused to have it applied. If Charlie and I had known, he would not have taken me into the oldest age. Faye played this either very arbitrarily or very underhandedly by not letting us know: It would have been easy for her to say stop, I'm stopping now, but she showed her contempt to all of us, and I got the feeling that though I had been looking bad, she wanted to make sure I looked a lot older than she ever would.)

I want to speak to Frank P. about the makeup difference. He is irritated and says I may speak to him when he has a minute. I wait. I try to calm myself. I explain to Frank. He says he is under so much pressure from the studio and has had to live with it since the second day of shooting, and that it would cost a hundred-and-fifty thousand to go into Thursday. They're a million dollars over budget already. If the age difference were so obvious—he didn't think it was, because it was a far shot—he will cut it. Something has to get cut out, he says—the film is running one hour over already. He could lose twenty minutes in tightening but forty minutes just has to go. Whole scenes will have to go, eventually. I tell him I hope I won't be cut out of the film. He says we'll just have to do with the old-age cheat. I say, well at least light me differently in the first one. He says he will and thanks me for being so adult about it. What else could I do? I couldn't win.

I am upset when I walk into the makeup trailer. Diana is there—she has been very emotional throughout the day. We all talk. Diana says Faye has changed so many of her scenes and that she is taking them over. Diana feels she didn't even get her coverage. Yeah, that sounds familiar! When she told Frank about Faye's domination, Frank said, "Oh no, I don't think so." Diana says she has been upset all day. Frank had upset her this morning when he said he didn't have time to discuss line changes. Vivienne says Frank does what Faye tells him to do. Charlie says he'd never work with him again. They don't like Frank P. Diana says Faye seems to be in competition with her, and that she's not really real—Faye doesn't know where the emotion comes from. Diana finds it hard to relate. She straightens up and says Ms. Sharaff said she had to really be strong.

We ride back together in the car. We're glad we spoke to each other and agree to use it in tomorrow's scene. Somewhere we'll use it. Diana says it's too bad Faye's not sympathetic. Also, it is strange that she took every curse word out. Joan cursed, especially in private—it would have been a nice contrast. We hug each other.

I come home. Richard's very strange—druggy, secretive. Refuses to talk, except to say he's leaving to go collect money people owe him. Find out he didn't have the three hundred and fifty he took out earlier. He says he loaned a hundred and fifty of it to his friend John. I don't believe him. He's a sneak, and I don't trust him anymore. This relationship is getting too painful. A lot of anger and rage on my part. I call Dr. Glass (my Reichian therapist) in New York. I'll have to make a decision on this very soon.

Wednesday, April 15th

Work at 6 a.m. I'm set ready at 8:30. Richard and I had a big fight on the way to work. Last night he came home while I was sleeping and wanted to talk to me. He confessed to cocaine and heroin use and lying to me and cheating from the check book, taking money and covering up. I was furious. But it flared up this morning. I have a lot of rage about this and so does Richard. He pounded the car so hard his hand bled. I went on to the set—and felt really bad. My real life is a mess. Let me run and be Carol Ann.

We shoot the scene with Faye and I watching Diana on T.V. accepting Joan's award. I finally got my first close-up. Then another.

Frank P. takes a Polaroid of him kissing me in my old-age makeup and shows it to Frank Y. I tell him he better not show it to his wife, Barbara, or he'll be in trouble. He says what about Richard? (I always felt during the shoot that there was a possibility of an affair with Frank Perry. We sought each other out almost every morning for that hug. He often told me that I had the most beautiful eyes and that he felt himself melt into them, then he wrote a wonderful note on my photo with him. It says, "Dearest Rutanya, my love, my heart, my true passion. Always, Frank

Perry, the handsome one." We both acted very professionally, yet we found a lot of solace in each other's company. I think if Frank really knew how unhappy I was in my personal life, maybe things would have been different, but he didn't know, I didn't tell him, and so he respected me.)

We talk about the scene when Faye gets the award from Diana in person, when Christina brings the award back to Joan, that is to be shot later. I mention the knitting choice. Faye says she didn't think I should be in the scene. What? Screw Carol Ann again? Oh yes, she doesn't want anyone but herself to have any film time, including me. Frank says to let him think about it. I say to myself and Charlie later that one close-up of me was enough for her. Charlie says she can't take the competition. But to my surprise and delight Frank P. does have me in there, throughout the whole scene. Frank finally stood up for me! I could have cried from happiness! It's clearer to me now than ever that Frank has been afraid of being fired by Faye. Or replaced, as they say. Now, with just a couple of days to go, it wouldn't happen and he was free to direct at last. (Except, you know, for all the late-phase budget and time constraints.)

Richard comes on set right after lunch. He cries, saying he was so frightened to tell me and feels really bad about it. He says he feels like a creep and liar. It is the truth at last.

I am the last to be shot after fourteen hours, again. But this time, I don't care, because I know I will be in the shot. I get a close-up and it went really well—I think one of my best scenes. It was full of feeling, truthful and emotional but understated, of me really listening to Faye and Diana. I feel this was some of my best and deepest work in the film. (It was cut.)

Finish at 8:10 p.m. Takes an hour to get my makeup off. No hot water. Charlie has to boil some in the prop room. Stop by Faye's trailer, since she'd asked me to stop by, and she gives me her phone number in New York. Why? I will never call her. Today she signed a lot of photos for the crew. They were really happy to get them. Funny, after all their complaints about her. Me too, I guess.

See David, who says I should not be seen talking to him, it drives Frank and Frank crazy. Meet David Koontz's son, David the Second. Diana is still upset about herself. She stopped her close-up twice on the line "I meant everything I said tonight, Mommie." It irritated Frank P. and later Faye said that Diana is strange tonight. Diana tells me that Faye told her to have a good life, family, et cetera, and to get out of the business. No wonder Diana was upset. I have a beer as we finish talking and Frank and Frank call me a lush.

Get home and hug Richard, even though I feel like hitting him hard, shower, wrap presents for the crew. Learn that the press party had been announced on T.V., as was its cancellation. Regis Philbin and all the press were to have been there. They were going to have all those pretty girls model Faye's clothes and show people around the sets, and close friends of Crawford, such as Cesar Romero, were to have been there, too. It would have been great to have talked with him. Faye wants no competition. Too bad.

Thursday, April 16th

Work call at 9 a.m. Twelve-hour turnaround. Charlie makes me up extra special, since he says he knows I will be photographed. Frank P. comes in to see how I am feeling and also to tell me that David Koontz gave an interview with this woman columnist that was in some paper today, about how the movie could be this or that—could go either way, or just be a runaway Dunaway picture, it would depend upon the integrity of Perry and Yablans. Frank is pissed. He says if he had nothing good to say, he shouldn't have said anything. Diana says she wants to add a little exchange between us about our relationship and also about how Joan is still dressing her daughter after all these years. (This was the scene where I bring her the dress to wear.) I agree, I think this is a good idea.

I give my gifts of little notebooks that I wrapped last night. Everyone is pleased. I'm glad I did it. Give Frank and Frank their photos. They love them. Frank P. writes, "The Four Mumsketeers," Franks Y. writes, "How to Finance a Film, or: The Mommie Dearest Caper," and "The Frank Yablans Repertory Company." They really love them. Paul Lohmann, the D.P., comes up and says put her camera away, she's too good, too good. What a compliment. Frank and Frank both want an additional photo of them together. It is part of the smaller photos I have also given them, but I tell them I'd also make up a set. They offer to pay me. I refuse. I also ask Frank Y. if I could have copies of some stills on the house. He says yes.

Mara is having her hair dyed back to brown. I remember when Vivienne complained about having to bleach her hair so much cause it grew out fast. She said why hadn't they hired an actress with real blonde hair? Frank P. tells everyone how Mara the real champion of the film.

Wait, did she just win the pissing contest?

We went to the set to rehearse the scene with me and Diana, when I bring her the dress. We work out some additional dialogue, drop the seamstress line, add "I'm going to miss you, Christina." Take my time—constantly making myself aware of not rushing. Charlie comes up and tells me not to move my neck so much, but to move it with arthritic condition side to side and when I look down, to look down with my shoulders. I first take it negatively, but quickly change to positive. I know he's trying to help me. Use it. I do it in the next take. Charlie says it was good. We've been having only one take—this once, two takes. We move back to cover the entire scene. It works so smoothly. Frank P. is singing Mairzy Doats and the crew and I join in. Frank says you have to be over fifty to know that one. Charlie says it seems like a different film out there today, so much more relaxed, and that's because Faye was wrapped. It's true, I feel that, too. Tension seems to have evaporated. We have to do the next to last scene thrice—once the camera is off, second time I have trouble with the door, third time's okay, although I worry about having done it too fast. Frank P. says no, it was fine.

The very last shot of the day and of the film is mine: A single on me watching Diana on the phone. We also do it three times. First time, Frank wants more emotion. Second time, he says it was too much. Third time's Goldilocks. That's it. Finished. John, the driver, comes over to say how good he thinks I was and to take a picture with me. We also take a group photo. I kiss Frank and Frank. New Terry, the replacement script person, says it was a lovely scene. I wish him well. He says it was hard coming in at the end. I understand. We go to take off my makeup. My face is really bruised.

I call Richard after. He says he doesn't want to come to the wrap party. Something is wrong, I can feel it. When I get home, he isn't there. I am upset. He comes in later with kitty litter. I sense something. I confront him again. This time he only denies it once and then admits it: He has taken heroin again. We have an emotional time and he asks me to forgive him. He's spent over a hundred on it today that I know of. I ask about the other night and find out he'd taken eight hundred and probably more from our account. (Thousands, I'd discover.) Richard's very emotional and angry—I am devastated by the betrayals.

We go to the wrap party at 8:30 p.m. Ralph Nelson, the still photographer, is upset. All of his hundred-plus careful shots of Faye were axed by Terry. Terry wanted exclusive stills. Eileen, Frank Y.'s assistant, says to talk to Frank Y. about it. They all hate Terry anyway, she says. (That goes back to the week at the beginning, when we thought the film might be canceled, because Faye had insisted Terry O'Neill be made co-producer or else she would walk. I heard Frank Yablans wanted to replace her because he hated being extorted, but the costumes were all bespoke and the camera tests had been done, so he was forced by the studio to concede.)

I am wearing my beautiful white suit, Richard his black suit. The place is full. There is a dance band, Western style. Stop at the bathroom and comb my hair. Everyone is surprised at how pretty I look. Frank P. says Lynn Stalmaster (famous casting director) should see my like this.

We meet Abe Polonsky (noted screenwriter) and Mrs. Polonsky, Terry O'Neill introduces us. Faye did not come. After Terry disappears, Abe says so now what's the real story? I say you mean the dish? His eyes twinkle, yes. I say it was Hell. He says people said Faye thought she had become Joan. Except the real Joan was loved by the crew, I say. Abe says the original script that Frank and Frank did was really good, he only polished it and filled in a few things.

Meet Ruth Yablans, Frank's wife. Frank Y. says this is the best work that I, Rutanya, have ever done, and that he is going to push me for an Oscar nomination for it. I say I'd love it, I'm not gonna lie. (Of course, a lot of Carol Ann wound up cut for time, to say nothing of our collective dashed Oscar dreams.)

Frank and Frank are presented the drawings, now framed, that we all signed. They love them. They describe them to the guests and make some wonderful comments. Frank P. says it was the hardest film he's ever done, but also the best. Frank Y. quips how this was the best-fed crew ever.

Later, Frank Y. sits with us eating around the table in Joan Crawford's living room set and someone says Frank's drunk a quart of whiskey. Frank says, "I'm depressed." Someone says Frank, there's a crisis. Frank says, "I'm not depressed anymore."

Richard and I are the first ones to dance on the dance floor and then other people follow. Richard gets teased for raising his hand when the bandleader asks if there are any chauvinists here. Betty's husband also raises his hand. Just the two of them. We dance a lot—fast and slow. At one point Diana and Frank Y. dance really dirty, like he was fucking her from the rear. Diana is really drunk. She came with one of her brothers. We talk to Frank P.'s wife, Barbara. She wonders when he is going to crash. We talk with her daughter, who lives in London. Frank Y. leaves and gives us both a hug. Then Frank P. leaves, too.

We leave around midnight. On the way out, we ran into Bernadene, Faye's costumer, who thanks me for all my support. (Support? I know some people weren't that nice to her because she was always with Faye, and later she had borne some of the blame for Ms. Sharaff's departure, but all I remember doing was struggling to remain neutral, which obviously meant a lot more than I realized.) We are both visibly surprised when she tells us she has two teenage sons—I'd always thought she was in her twenties.

We walk back to the car. Head to Joe Allen's for cappuccino. People stare at us. We close the place down and go home. Everyone was drunk, the whole world was drunk, and I was sober.

Life after Dearest
1982 - 2015

UNTIL FAYE CONTACTED my theatrical agency when she heard I was publishing my diary, the last time I heard from her was shortly after *Mommie Dearest*. She was doing William Alfred's "The Curse of an Aching Heart" on Broadway and she phoned me at home to ask for my acting teacher, Paul Mann's, number. Paul had been in charge of the acting program when she was a member of the Lincoln Center Repertory Theater. Faye was opening in three days and was having problems with her role.

I stood in line and bought a ticket, as she did not offer me a comp, and went backstage after to say hello. Terry O'Neill was controlling access. "Oh, you're okay, Rutanya. Faye would like to see you." I was shown to her room, where she received me. We spoke briefly about *Mommie* and Faye said, "Oh, I'll get a[n Oscar] nomination, but I won't win. It's just too controversial." Sadly, no one did—I honestly think at the least the set designer, Richard

Goddard, should have been nominated, as well as Irene Sharaff for costumes. I liked Faye's memorable performance, too. She made bold choices and followed through with them. I just wish she hadn't boldly chosen to treat it like a one-woman show.

I spoke to Paul later in class and he said he had gone down to sit in on a rehearsal, then asked her, "Why didn't you call me earlier? It's impossible to change much two days before you open." He said he told her that she was playing the woman as someone who is complaining about life. Instead, she should be a woman who is speaking for life. However, Paul did say that she roller-skated well. "The Curse" closed after a month.

People have asked me many times why Faye hasn't wanted to be associated with *Mommie Dearest* in any way, even in interviews. I have answered, "She just doesn't have a sense of humor," but I think it's deeper than that, she needs to be Number One. She cannot subject herself to be second banana to Joan Crawford, and that is what she feels she would be doing at *Mommie Dearest* events. She as a person would have to be greater than Joan, but she can't be in this fandom. Ultimately, Joan is the star still adored by so many fans—it will always be Joan whom they love, not her.

Of course, there also seems to be a more general personality problem. When Faye appeared on *Inside the Actors Studio*, she told James Lipton that others didn't like working with her because she was a perfectionist. Earlier in my career, I witnessed Barbra Streisand abuse people on her movie sets—now she too claims in interviews that she was disliked because she was a perfectionist. No, Barbra, no, Faye, you were disliked because you were abusers. A perfectionist ought to be someone who sees perfection and finds perfection around them; it's the imperfectionists like Faye and Barbra who keep looking for the imperfection until they find it, for what we focus on, we will find. Why demand perfection if you can't offer it? I think that *Mommie Dearest* has too many imperfections with which she'd have to coexist—and own some of the responsibility for.

One more thing: I remember a brief conversation I had with Faye in the middle of shooting, which is not in my diary. Somehow the subject of face-lifts and plastic surgery came up. Faye was adamant that she would never have any.

I know I was not the only one to suffer on that set. I also forgot to diary this because I must have been exhausted and stressed, but I remember holding Diana Scarwid in the Van Ness parking lot at Paramount while she cried after an extremely long day and late night of shooting. She was so very unhappy working with Faye and it just all came out with sobs and tears. Faye was really mean to Diana and she was miserable. I held her and let her cry. My only advice to her was to use it in her work, to use all these thoughts and feelings that she had right now, because I am certain they were similar to those Christina experienced.

I did not see Diana afterward for a long time. I understand that she did move back to Savannah, Georgia, and had two children, while maintaining a career. She continues to do good work. I last saw Diana when we did the DVD interviews that were in the "Hollywood Royalty" edition. She still looks so lovely.

I last saw Mara Hobel several years ago at the *Mommie Dearest* Mothers' Day event in New York City's Town Hall. The real Christina was there, too, for book signing. Lypsinka, also known as the great John Epperson, gave a brilliant drag performance as Joan, and that was where I first publicly read from my diary to a wild crowd. I didn't recognize Mara: She was a lovely, grown-up woman, a mother herself, no longer the little girl I knew.

I became better friends with David Koontz and Christina Crawford after the film finished. They generously hosted Richard and me in their lovely home in Tarzana, California, on several occasions. David and Richard played pool and had a lot of fun together. Christina was not involved with making the *Mommie Dearest* film, so it was there that I really got to know her as a very smart and articulate woman with a beautiful smile.

It's also where I did a bad thing. Once, when David and Christina had to go away on a business meeting to raise some money to try and adapt another of Christina's books to film, in which she would star, Richard and I took care of their cat, Copper, and dogs, Prince, Princess, and Sundance. I just couldn't resist the temptation of peeking in Christina's closet. I know I shouldn't have—and maybe I shouldn't share this—but everything I saw was on wire hangers, left from the cleaners. At last, I knew.

I observed a few other "callbacks." Like Joan, Christina kept an immaculate house. She also had a beautiful rose garden in her backyard and shared Joan's passion and talent for fabulous knitting. Her love of dogs, I assume, was also influenced by her mother, though none of Joan's dogs or her other two children are depicted in the film.

On another occasion, when we were staying with them as I was shooting a 7-Up commercial on location with the great director Leslie Dektor, Richard let Kukums out into the Tarzana countryside after he scratched and meowed incessantly at the door around five in the morning. It was the last time we saw Kukums. Richard was racked with guilt, but I couldn't blame him—Kukums liked to be outdoors and was like a little dog because when I called him he would run back right away when called. We didn't know there were coyotes in Los Angeles. We spent forever searching the grounds and pounds on the off chance we could find him, but never did. Rest in peace, my dear baby.

David and I have remained friends all these years after their divorce. He moved to Key West, Florida, where he met and married his wife, Carol. David is now in the mortgage business and continues to write scripts. In fact, David wrote the original screenplay adaption of *Mommie Dearest*, but isn't credited, as the final script was completely revised by a number of other credited and uncredited writers, including Frank Perry, Frank Yablans, Robert Getchell, Tracy Hotchner, and Abraham Polonsky. Christina moved to Idaho and still lives there, though I see her when she happens to be in New York, such as when she starred in the one-woman multi-media show, "Surviving Mommie Dearest."

As hard as it was for those involved to see what came of our great visions for the film, I can only imagine Christina and David going to see it in Los Angeles soon after it premiered and watching it in an otherwise deserted theater. It must be very painful, as David Colman thought in *The New York Times*, to see your hard childhood distorted and made into a camp folly. And yet, Christina has had fun with the film's legacy over the years, such as having Lypsinka take part in her anniversary celebration for her book, further illustrating her resilience.

She has also since clarified to me some rumors about production: Christina never visited the set, never met Faye, never met Mara, and recalls meeting Diana only after she finished shooting. Fans might also find it interesting to know that it was Betty Barker—Joan's longtime personal secretary and a historical source of the amalgamated character of Carol Ann—as well as a driver and armed guard who picked up Christina on the way home from Chadwick. Joan wasn't there. Christina said to me that she and her brother detested Betty: "She lied about us and was always making trouble." Overall, the film's a wildly different telling of Christina's experience. If you want to know her story, read *Mommie Dearest*, a classic that forever changed the dialogue about domestic violence and child abuse in America.

Frank Perry did four more films before he died on August 29, 1995, in New York City, from prostate cancer. In 1985, he cast a film called *Compromising Positions* in New York, in which were quite a few roles for women. I called his office and his assistant answered. I left a message for Frank to call me. When I had not heard back a few days later, I called again and left another message. The assistant called me back and told me Frank had gotten my message. No personal returned phone call ever. That's Hollywood.

Frank Yablans produced eleven films after Mommie Dearest and started his own production company, Promenade Pictures, with a focus on Biblical and "family-values" entertainment. His last film was the animated *Noah's Ark: The New Beginning* (2012), starring Michael Keaton, before Frank died on November 27, 2014. I will always remember him as a class act. He graciously said of me in the "Hollywood Royalty" edition of *Mommie*: "In anything I do, there is room for Rutanya, she is a generous actress. A generous actress is somebody who will go underneath, who will allow somebody to take center stage, but without this person you'll disappear at center stage, and she has that ability. She's a remarkable woman."

Irene Sharaff died on August 10, 1993, in New York City. She truly had a genius eye for costumes and fabrics, and such a dignified presence that, though I loved working with her, I've never felt it proper to call her Irene. I rang her in New York after *Mommie*, as she had given me her phone number, and she returned my call. I was doing *Vigilante* (1983), low budget, and I asked her advice on where to look for some wardrobe that wouldn't cost a lot, and she pointed me in a few directions. Unfortunately, I never spoke with her again, but I had met Ms. Sharaff earlier when I photo doubled for Barbra Streisand in a beautiful costume and hat that she designed for *Hello, Dolly!* (1969). I remember Ms. Sharaff fussing over me to make sure I looked good and she was so happy that her costume fit me so well. Another costume I wore as a townsperson on it was one that Judy Garland wore in *Meet Me in St. Louis* (1944). It's slate gray, with a yellow under-blouse and tassels, and fit me perfectly, accompanied with little lace-up boots. I saw that costume when it went on display at a Beverly Hills auction house a couple of years ago, selling for thousands of dollars. I had worn it for weeks. And in doing research for this book, I learned that Ms. Sharaff also designed the costumes for *Meet Me in St. Louis*, including, presumably, that dress. Truly a remarkable career. I never told her that we had worked together before *Mommie*, because I felt it trivial and knew she wouldn't remember me—now I'm sorry I didn't mention our connection.

Charles Schram died on November 14, 2008, at the age of 97, in Simi Valley, California. He supervised makeup on *Grease 2* (1982) and worked on two TV productions in '83 before he went back into the retirement he had postponed to do *Mommie*.

Vivienne Walker died on September 3, 2009, in Los Angeles. She did three more films after *Mommie Dearest*, including *Grease 2* with Charlie, before she retired. She was an animal lover and had several dogs and cats, one being a black and white cat that had a little mustache she got such a kick out of. I visited her several times through the years and she was always so kind and lovely to me. I remember her having an O'Keefe and Merritt stove, an old one from maybe the '40s or '50s—immaculate. She said she had looked at that stove for months in a store window and when she had saved enough money, she bought it. I brought my son, Jeremy, on several of these visits and she was always so nice, showing us her beautiful orchid garden in the back, where she grew so many beautiful, rare varieties, and sending Jeremy twenty dollars every Christmas. Jeremy would write thank you notes to "Auntie Viv" in return.

Of all the people on *Mommie*, I remained closest to Vivienne. She was a great woman. I will never forget a story she told me of when she worked with Merle Oberon in London. It was in the '30s or '40s. Ms. Oberon had an Indian woman with her, whom she introduced to everyone as her maid—however, the woman was really Ms. Oberon's mother. At that time in the British film industry, she could not be known as being part Indian, so her "maid" constantly traveled with her. (Imagine if Carol Ann were Joan's unwed, unacknowledged teenage mother. That would certainly give the aging incongruity a plausible backstory.) Vivienne worked with the biggest female stars of the '30s through the '80s. She would always tell me how wonderful Joan was to her, always sending her holiday cards, birthday cards, and calling her personally several times a year. She detested the way Joan was depicted in *Mommie Dearest*.

We last saw Sam Peckinpah shortly before his death in '84. We met at his room in the Algonquin. He was directing two Julian Lennon music videos and was deeply unhappy about it, but needed the money. He said he wanted to get back to finishing up a movie script, in which both of us would have parts. I still wonder what he had in mind. Something most fans probably don't know is that Sam's favorite film of his, he told me, was *The Ballad of Cable Hogue* (1970), a romantic dramedy. It is a great and sweet film, definitely worth a watch. His nephew, David Peckinpah, whom we knew well, wrote me a letter in '88, in which he said:

Sam was very fond of you and Richard ... It's a damn shame he flamed out so early, but in retrospect, it might have been his time. As you know, he lived for the business, and the money men had all but abandoned him toward the end. He was being offered only shit, and I doubt things would have changed. He was incredibly talented, but unfortunately, even more self-destructive. He battled his addictions all his life, and never could get the upper hand. I was following in his footsteps in all areas ... his death snapped me out of it and put me in touch with the reality of the destructive power of substances. I've been in A.A. for a little over a year now, and have never felt more creative. I'm only sorry that Sam couldn't have found the release from the demons that I have. No guarantees it will last forever, but a day at a time is all it takes.

David died in 2006 of a drug overdose.

Warren Miller tried very, very hard to be a successful actor and screenwriter. Like with so many others, fame eluded him.

Steve Forrest died on May 18, 2012, in Thousand Oaks, California. Steve was a joy to work with. He was always polite and fun and just didn't care about what Faye thought or didn't think. He spent his time on the set with the rest of us and always had a good time. Steve was one of those people with whom I would have loved to have done a series, as it would have been wonderful to work with him every week.

Conversely, even though a lot of years have passed since I last saw him, I still harbor a great deal of anger at Paul Jenkins for enabling and supplying drugs to Richard over the years. In fact, I remember only one time that I ever liked Paul: We drove him to see his son's rock band play at a venue in Santa Monica. Paul was so happy and infectiously proud of him. We, of course, still wound up paying the bill. Very Paul. When Richard and I were in Los Angeles a few years after *Mommie Dearest*, we saw Paul wandering the streets. He said he had no place to stay, he was homeless. We took him back to the Magic Castle, where we were staying, and paid for a room for him. The next day we wound up with his four hundred dollar phone bill. We told him we can't afford this and I told him "Paul, you need help." Richard and I took him to Cedars-Sinai Hospital, where at that time the Thalians—a mental health charity founded by actors—had a special unit for actors that was free. He was admitted. We visited him a number of times there, and he actually gained weight and looked good. Very un-Paul. I used the initials Paul J. throughout the original diary to conceal his identity—I was planning to keep it that way for publication, before I learned that Paul had died in 2013.

The '80s were a time when heroin addiction had to stay hidden and secretive. Cocaine was acceptable, but heroin made you a monster, like therapy made you "crazy." There was very little out there in terms of treatment or support. The Reagan years were a terrible time for health care, mental and physical—as his administration deconstructed the already-tenuous mental health system and demonized addiction, Reagan deliberately and totally ignored the AIDS explosion until '87, which further stigmatized heroin users, given that HIV can be transmitted through shared needles and crazy ideas of how easy it was to catch had become normal discourse, stuff you'd teach your kids.

A few expensive opiate clinics had cropped up to profit from the dearth of care, but we could not afford them. Out of desperation for help we went to the Actors Fund for support. The Actors Fund is supposed to help actors in crisis and Richard always had a percentage of his check go to it. It had a very healthy endowment. We begged them to save Richard's life by giving him a chance to go get help at a live-in clinic for a year. They turned us down. His life didn't seem to matter to them. They would sit on their millions. I never supported the Actors Fund again.

When Philip Seymour Hoffman died of heroin addiction in 2014, there was an outpouring of grief. His death was tragic and I felt so deeply for his family. I also felt that his death finally took the taboo off of heroin, helped humanize the tragedy of it. You could still be a human being, a great talent, a father, famous, respected, accomplished, and be suffering from heroin addiction.

Even at his worst self, Richard was a good friend to a lot of people. I remember one evening he and Ray Sharkey came in looking wasted. Ray, a talented actor, worked steadily in films and television series; he won a Golden Globe for Best Actor and starred in his own short-lived ABC sitcom. They were two boys from Brooklyn and two heroin addicts entangled in each other's lives, hanging out with each other most of the year. I'd come to despise Ray, although I think that was mostly anger transference.

"I'm so hungry," Ray pleaded.

I reluctantly threw some spaghetti into a pot, topped it with fridge-cold sauce, and dropped the plate on his lap. He slurped at it until it was just a saucy plate, which he licked clean. "This is the best pasta I've ever had."

Astonished, I looked at him, almost feeling guilty that I didn't warm up the sauce. He seemed sincerely grateful. We were all silent for an uncomfortably long time before Richard spoke.

"Ray, Ray, you gotta stop the stuff. Do you want to wind up to be a fifty-year-old drug addict like me?" But Ray never got to fifty. He died of complications resulting from AIDS in 1993, likely from sharing all those needles—Ray's drug habit had escalated to four hundred dollars a day.

Richard died before his time in February, 2006, hit by a bus that was rushing to ferry people to Atlantic City casinos while he legally crossed West Eighty-Sixth Street to eat at his favorite diner.

Among others, Al Pacino sent a dear letter to be read in eulogy, that I'll share because he says a lot and says it well:

> *I am saddened by Richard's passing.*
> *The first time I ever saw Richard was in a play we did together at the New Dramatist. He was in his early twenties. I was struck by his intensity and power of his acting. We all looked up to him as the next Dean or Brando. He had some early success but nothing that ever matched his huge gifts. I often wondered about Richard and how he never got a chance to really communicate and demonstrate the range of his great emotions and sensibility. He was by far the actor of his generation. And, as the saying goes, "there are no small parts, only small actors." Richard Bright changed all that. He did not get enough parts that could compare with the size of his talent. It's written all over his screen performances.*
> *I had the good fortune to see him in a play at St. Clemens Church many years ago, where he did have a so-called vehicle and it is a performance that will live in my memory as one of the greatest I have ever seen. Suffice it to say, what he did contribute to the field of acting in general was both poignant and admirable. He never felt he was too good for the role. His eloquence and performance in* Billy the Kid, The Getaway, Panic in Needle Park, *and also* The Godfather(s) *demonstrates what he was able to do to make and give a movie the kind of gravity and reality that makes them special. Richie was special. The kind of person you never meet. A Brooklyn boy from President Street. Tough, smart, but most of all, an artist.*
> *I will always remember his wildness, his unconventional approach, his individuality, his intelligence, and finally, his work.*
> *Much love and affection for a great actor,*
>   —Al

Richard never escaped drugs. Spiritual author Eckhart Tolle wrote, "Every addiction arises from an unconscious refusal to face and move through your own pain. Every addiction starts with pain and ends with pain. Whatever the substance you are addicted to—alcohol, food, legal or illegal drugs, or a person—you are using something or someone to cover up your pain." I feel this could have been written for Richard, and I empathize with his constant suffering, but the ups and downs of addiction also take a miserable toll on family and, unable to heal his pain, I finally decided I had to do something about mine. Richard and I separated in 1990. It took a long while for us to learn how to be friends again. I left with an empty bank account, our two-year-old son in one arm and our cat, Kukums III, in the other, flying back to Los Angeles on a prayer and a credit card in hope of a miracle.

As soon as I finished *Mommie Dearest*, my agent, Kendall, set up an appointment for me with some top publicity people. She felt that it would be good for my career to have some good publicity coverage, but I had no money left to make it happen, which has always been a big regret in my life, as good and calculated P.R. has helped build and sustain practically every big artist's career. Insofar as my exposure went, I did get called to do a lot of elderly grandmother auditions thanks to the aging makeup, all of which would go along the lines of, "Who are you? Oh, we thought you were old. You're much too young for this," and sometimes, by way of apology, "We can't afford that kind of makeup."

The principal exception was when I was being pushed for the role of Dolores Montelli in *Amityville II* (1982) and had to be approved by the producer, Dino De Laurentiis. He spoke very little—in English, at least, which he seemed to pretend he couldn't speak. He had a very formidable presence, stern and seated behind an extra-large desk with the casting director at his side. Italian flowed back and forth. The only words I understood were *Deer Hunter* and *Mommie Dearest—Mommie Dearest, Mommie Dearest, Mommie Dearest*. I did my best to keep calm and smile. He approved the screen test, which went great, all one take, and I hurried to have coffee with Richard and tell him the good news. He was late, so I called my answering service and received an urgent message, not from him, but from the casting office. It seemed they had lost sound on my take and I had to reshoot it immediately. I hurried straight back. The reshoot went well, but I still worried because the first time was better.

We filmed the exteriors in what is now Toms River, New Jersey, and then were flown to Mexico City, where all of the interiors were built at Churubusco Studios. I was on the film for about two months, during which my father died in Riga, and because it was during the Soviet era they required two weeks to get a visa, so there was no way I could go to the funeral. I was unable to sleep for a week and when I finally crashed, it was for the whole weekend. A week later, Burt Young's father died, too. We formed a real bond then and there.

I told Jack Magner, my co-star who was hoping for a breakthrough in this film, that it may or may not happen and to be in it for the long haul, though Jack, for his own reasons, would opt out of his acting career a few years later. Maye, his wife, had come down to stay during the shooting of the film and we became friends. One morning, I woke up remembering a dream of looking for Maye's obituary in *The New York Times*. Her name wasn't there, and I said "We still have time." Maye had been having serious pain in her abdomen, but she thought it was just bad menstrual cramps. Very shaken by my dream, I immediately called Maye's room. She answered and said she was feeling worse. I said I am taking you to the hospital, delaying just to inform the production office. We got to the hospital just in time: Maye's appendix had burst and blood poisoning had already begun. After there was nothing left for me to do at the hospital, I went to the set to tell Jack and assure him that Maye would be all right. He got permission to leave and we went back to the hospital together. She recovered in a week and stayed until the end of the shoot.

On my first day off after that, I wanted to go to see Trotsky's house, now a museum. Trotsky was—I had heard in hushed fragments from my grandmother—a friend of my grandfather, as they had both been comrades of Lenin and taken part in the Revolution, traveling and rallying the people. I took an hour-long taxi ride to what were then the outskirts of Mexico City and toured the house, where I saw the blood-spattered glasses that had fallen and cracked on Trotsky's desk when the assassin's axe hit his head. It was a walk back in time and I was enthralled: Here was a connection with my grandfather. The house was left entirely as it was during Trotsky's time living there. After I spent some hours looking and sitting in the garden, it was late afternoon and I looked for a taxi back. There were none, so I walked and walked and walked, and then realized I wasn't even positive about my direction. I started to panic as the sun went down. Finally I found a cab and gave thanks when I got back to the hotel.

There was a lot more that happened on that shoot and others, and a lot more happened in the years before and since, but I'll save those stories for another time, less I lose the thread of this one. Frank Yablans summarized *Mommie Dearest* in the "Hollywood Royalty" edition as an "audience movie, audiences like to interact with the film," and I am constantly amazed at the number of people, particularly within the LGBT+ community, that adore, participate in, and keep alive the movie. It has a following stronger now than when the film opened, and frankly it took those subsequent thirty or so years for me to start to realize that real, enduring interest.

In 1998, as mentioned, Christina invited me, other cast members, and John Epperson's Joan-esque drag character, the great Lypsinka, to her book's twenty-fifth anniversary event at Manhattan's Town Hall. I was astonished by the audience's response—the full house gave me the then-biggest ovation of my life—as well as and their interest in my personal experience and recollections, when I read briefly from the diary for the first time in public. Until that night, I didn't think anyone would have much cared. Then came more invites: To appear with Steven Polito's brilliantly funny drag character Hedda Lettuce at a celebratory Mother's Day interactive riffing at the Ziegfeld Theatre, where more than a thousand people sent "love waves" my way for several solid minutes; to fly to Denver as the Public Library's guest for a wonderful, fun *Mommie Dearest* Mother's Day event; again with Hedda at the sold-out Clearview Cinema in Manhattan; and to a true and packed and frenzied gala produced by Marc Huestis at San Francisco's historic Castro Theatre, where I got my wakeup call when about two thousand people cheered and humbled me as I read from my diary. People wanted to know. They were interested in what my experience had been, and they wanted me to share it.

But in doing so, I also had to share my own life during those four months, if I were to be true to the diary, which scared me. I kept a diary to keep my sanity, and it was a way to express my thoughts and try to comprehend what was happening, to give myself some focus and clarity throughout a turbulent shoot and an emotionally difficult period of my life. However, my life and my life as Carol Ann were intertwined; one would not leave the other alone to simply be for those four months. Most of the time, actors go in for a day, a week, or a few weeks. To have been on for the entire shoot was an experience I hadn't had before and to have been on a shoot this turbulent was also new. So, I needed strength and order.

But we can't afford to retreat from our lives, past or present. We go on, even if we don't have the power to change it and, if necessary, somehow muddle through it all, remembering that our lives ought to be valued and loved, above all by ourselves. That has taken me years to learn, and I hope you have or will, too. I was reminded of this when Faye, from whom I had not heard in thirty-plus years, and who has famously and dramatically disowned the film to the point of shutting down interviews when the subject arises, e-mailed my theatrical agent twice about contacting her right away. I had just submitted a draft of this work to publishers, and I felt the timing couldn't be coincidental. Maybe a publisher had contacted her people to say, "We think a *Mommie Dearest* book would sell better if Ms. Dunaway wrote it. She did keep a diary, too, didn't she? She didn't? Well, no matter, we have many talented ghostwriters on staff." I could imagine that, but I couldn't imagine what she wanted to talk to me about. I was dealing with a lot in my life at the moment as well as processing all the emotions of reliving my *Mommie Dearest* experiences and did not want to deal with Faye then, too, so I asked someone to inquire. He said he spent an hour on the phone with Faye and that she asked who was publishing my book, if he had read it, and if I could fly to Los Angeles at my expense to help her write her new book about the making of *Mommie Dearest*. My reward was to be acknowledged in it.

I was stunned. Could I have ever imagined this happening? Could I allow myself to be so undervalued again? Well, thank you, but no thank you. She can read my diary if she needs a refresher. I will look forward to reading her memoir.

"I shall raise my glass never to Ms. Faye Dunaway, never, never ... She is the most incredibly inconsiderate woman I have ever worked with ... They should have charged her for the cost of a day."

– Bette Davis on *The Gary Collins Show*

Made in the USA
Columbia, SC
19 September 2021